CONTENTS

TESTS	1
ANSWER KEY TO THE TESTS	56
ANSWER KEY TO THE STUDENT BOOK EXERCISES	73
WEBSITES	110

Tests

Tests have been provided for each chapter. You may select whole tests or parts of tests to evaluate your students. Each chapter test has three parts.

1. **Vocabulary.** This part of the test targets students' comprehension of content-specific and academic vocabulary. It is a modified cloze test based on an excerpt from the Introductory Reading. Ten words have been deleted from the passage; 12 words have been provided.

2. **Reading Comprehension.** This part of the test targets students' reading comprehension of a passage from the Main Reading. In this section, students are instructed to highlight important ideas; in Chapters 3 through 10, students are also instructed to annotate the text. The reading passage is followed by multiple choice questions and/or a matching exercise, open-ended questions, and a text organization task. The organization task instructs students to create a flow chart, diagram, time line, outline, or concept map based on the reading.

3. **Writing about Figures.** This part of the test targets students' ability to write about figures and photos, and to demonstrate their understanding of vocabulary and content. A vocabulary list is provided to facilitate their work. Depending on the strengths of the students in your class, you may wish to make this part of the test an open book test.

The vocabulary in every part of the tests has been drawn from the word form charts and from the lists of content-specific vocabulary and academic vocabulary in the follow-up section at the end of each chapter. Consequently, students should be encouraged to review the vocabulary in the Word Forms and Follow-up Assignments sections of a chapter as part of their preparation for a test.

Although the tests have three sections, students should be encouraged to think of them holistically. The vocabulary and reading comprehension sections provide a partial review of the chapter, and give students information they can draw on as they write about figures in the third section.

Points have not been allocated to any part of the tests to allow flexibility in weighting and scoring according to criteria you set for your class.

Name: _____ Date: _____

CHAPTER ONE TEST

Vocabulary

Complete the passage below with words from the following list. Use each word only once. You will not use all the words.

adaptive	exploiting	motivations	species
behavior	inflexible	predators	survive
dominance	modifying	respond	value

Understanding Behavior

When you watch a bird or squirrel, its activities appear to have a purpose. Birds search for food, take flight as you approach, and build nests in which to raise young. Usually the nests are inconspicuous or placed in difficult-to-reach spots. Likewise, squirrels collect and store nuts and acorns, "scold" you when you get too close, and learn to visit sites where food is available. All of these activities are (1) _____ and help the (2) _____ survive. Birds that do not take flight at the approach of another animal will be eaten by (3) _____. Squirrels that do not remember the location of sources of food will be less likely to (4) _____, and birds that build obvious nests on the ground will be more likely to lose their young to predators. However, we need to take care not to attach too much meaning to what animals do. They may not have the same "thoughts" and (5) _____ we do.

(6) _____ is how an organism acts, what it does, and how it does it. When we think about the behavior of an animal, we should keep in mind that behavior is like any other characteristic displayed by an animal. Behavior has a (7) _____ or significance to the animal as it goes about (8) _____ resources and reproducing more of its own species. Behavior is a very important part of the ecological role of any animal. It allows animals to escape predators, seek out mates, gain (9) _____ over others of the same species, and (10) _____ to changes in the environment.

Reading Comprehension

Read the passage below. As you read, highlight the important ideas and vocabulary used to express those ideas. Then do the test exercises that follow.

Instinctive Behavior and Learned Behavior

We need to discuss how animals generate specific behaviors and the two major kinds of behaviors: instinctive and learned. Both instinct and learning are involved in the behavior patterns of most organisms. We recognize **instinctive behavior** as behavior that is inborn, automatic, and inflexible, whereas **learning** requires experience and produces behaviors that can be changed. Most animals have a high proportion of instinctive behavior and very little learning; some, like many birds and mammals, are able to demonstrate a great deal of learned behavior.

Instinctive behaviors are automatic, preprogrammed, and genetically determined. Such behaviors are found in a wide range of organisms from simple one-celled protozoans to complex vertebrates. These behaviors are performed correctly the first time without previous experience when the proper stimulus is given. A *stimulus* is some change in the internal or external environment of the organism that causes it to react. The reaction of the organism to the stimulus is called a *response*.

The drawback of instinctive behavior is that it cannot be modified when a new situation presents itself, but it can be very effective for the survival of a species if it is involved in fundamental, essential activities that rarely require modification. Instinctive behavior is most common in animals that have short life cycles, simple nervous systems, and little contact with parents. Over long periods of evolutionary time, these genetically determined behaviors have been selected for and have been useful to most of the individuals of the species.

The alternative to preprogrammed, instinctive behavior is learned behavior. **Learning** is a change in behavior as a result of experience. Learning becomes more significant in long-lived animals that care for their young. Animals that live many years are more likely to benefit from an ability to recognize previously encountered situations and modify their behavior accordingly. Furthermore, because the young spend time with their parents they can imitate their parents and develop behaviors that are appropriate to local conditions. These behaviors take time to develop but have the advantage of adaptability. In order for learning to become a dominant feature of an animal's life, the animal must also have a large brain to store the new information it is learning. This is probably why learning is a major part of life for only a few kinds of animals like the vertebrates. In humans, it is clear that nearly all behavior is learned. Even such important behaviors as walking, communicating, and feeding oneself must be learned.

A Circle the correct answers.

1. Why are instinctive behaviors inflexible?

    a. because animals are simple and cannot think or change what they do

    b. because instinctive behaviors are very simple responses to specific stimuli

    c. because they usually involve basic behaviors that are essential to an organism's survival

2. Which one of the following is an example of a stimulus?

    a. A goose sitting on a nest of eggs falls asleep.

    b. A goose sitting on a nest of eggs sees a baseball near its nest.

    c. A goose sitting on a nest of eggs lays another egg.

3. In humans, why is walking categorized as a learned behavior, and not as an instinctive behavior?

   a. because humans have to spend time practicing walking

   b. because humans do not have many instinctive behaviors

   c. because humans are very small and weak when they are born

B Read the animal activities in the following chart. Decide whether each animal's behavior is instinctive or learned, and explain the value of these instinctive and learned behaviors as explained in the reading.

Activity	Explanation of the Value of the Animals' Instinctive / Learned Behavior
1. In a park, a squirrel sees a man sitting on a bench eating, and approaches him.	
2. In a nest, a bird's eggs hatch. As soon as the babies chirp and open their mouths, the adult bird feeds them.	
3. A herd of elephants uses a particular watering hole. When the water dries up in the summer heat, the elephants walk twenty miles to another watering hole.	
4. When a turtle's head is touched, the turtle pulls its head into its shell.	

C On a separate piece of paper, create a chart or diagram to illustrate the information in the reading. Provide a title for your chart or diagram.

Writing about Figures

Examine the figures below. Write a paragraph in which you identify and describe the types of behavior represented in each photograph and explain your reasons for your decisions. A vocabulary list has been provided. Choose words you need from the list.

adapt	habituation	instinct	significance
association	imprinting	modify	species
automatic	inflexible	organism	stimulus
explore	insight	response	value

A bird building a nest

A baby girl playing with a harmless Indigo snake

Name: _____ Date: _____

CHAPTER TWO TEST

Vocabulary

Complete the passage below with words from the following list. Use each word only once. You will not use all the words.

components	innate	isolated	species
exploit	instinct	refinements	vertebrates
imitate	invertebrates	scarce	whereas

Instinct and Learning Compared

It is important to recognize that all animals have both learned and instinctive behaviors and that one behavior may have elements that are both instinctive and learned. For example, biologists have raised song sparrows in the absence of any adult birds so there was no song for the young birds to (1) _____. These (2) _____ birds would sing a series of notes similar to the normal song of the (3) _____, but not exactly correct. Birds from the same nest that were raised with their parents developed a song nearly identical to that of their parents. If bird songs were totally instinctive, there would be no difference between these two groups. It appears that the basic melody of the song was inherited by the birds and that the (4) _____ of the song were the result of experience. Therefore, the characteristic song of that species was partly learned behavior (a change in behavior as a result of experience) and partly unlearned (instinctive). This is probably true of the behavior of many organisms; they show complex behaviors that are a combination of (5) _____ and learning. It is important to note that many kinds of birds learn most of their songs with very few (6) _____ components. For example, mockingbirds are very good at imitating the songs of a wide variety of bird species found in their local region.

This mixture of learned and instinctive behavior is not the same for all species. Many (7) _____ (e.g., insects) rely on instinct for the majority of their behavior patterns, (8) _____ many of the (9) _____ (particularly birds and mammals) use a great deal of learning. Typically the learned (10) _____ of an animal's behavior have particular value for the animal's survival. Most of the behavior of a honeybee is instinctive, but it is able to learn new routes to food sources. The style of nest built by a bird is instinctive, but the skill with which it builds may improve with experience.

6 Tests © 2005 by Lorraine C. Smith. Duplication for classroom use is permitted.

Reading Comprehension

Read the passage below. As you read, highlight the important ideas and vocabulary used to express those ideas. Then do the test exercises that follow.

Instinct and Learning in the Same Organism

As we saw in Chapter 1, scientists separate learned behavior into several categories, including association, imprinting, and insight.

Associative learning is extremely common in humans. We associate smells with certain kinds of food, sirens with emergency vehicles, and words with their meanings. Much of the learning that we do is by association. We also often use positive and negative reinforcement as ways to change behavior. We seek to reward appropriate behavior and punish inappropriate behavior. Much of the positive and negative reinforcement can be accomplished without having the actual experience because we can visualize possible consequences of our behavior. Adults routinely describe consequences for children so that children will not experience particularly harmful effects.

Imprinting in humans is more difficult to demonstrate, but there are some instances in which imprinting may be taking place. *Bonding* between mothers and infants is thought to be an important step in the development of the mother-child relationship. Most mothers form very strong emotional attachments to their children and, likewise, the children are attached to their mothers, sometimes literally, as they seek to maintain physical contact with their mothers. However, it is very difficult to show what is actually happening at this early time in the life of a child.

Insight is what our species prides itself on. We are thinking animals. *Thinking* is a mental process that involves memory, a concept of self, and an ability to reorganize information. We come up with new solutions to problems. We invent new objects, new languages, new cultures, and new challenges to solve. However, how much of what we think is really completely new, and how much is imitation? As mentioned earlier, association is a major core of our behavior, but we are also able to use past experiences, stored in our large brains, to provide clues to solving new problems.

For an animal to be successful, it must receive sufficient resources to live and reproduce. Therefore, organisms have many kinds of behaviors that divide, or allocate, the available resources so that the species as a whole is benefitted, even though some individuals may be harmed. One kind of behavior pattern that is often tied to successful reproduction is territorial behavior. A territory is the space used for food, mating, or other purposes, that an animal defends against others of the same species. The behaviors involved in securing and defending the territory are called **territorial behaviors**. A territory has great importance because it reserves exclusive rights to the use of a certain space for an individual.

When territories are first being established, there is much conflict between individuals. This eventually gives way to the use of a series of signals that define the territory and communicate to others that the territory is occupied. The male redwing blackbird has red shoulder patches, but the female does not. The male will perch on a high spot, flash his red shoulder patches, and sing to other males that happen to venture into his territory. Most other males get the message and leave his territory; those that do not leave, he attacks. After the territorial boundaries are established, little time is required to prevent other males from venturing close.

With many kinds of animals the possession of a territory is often a requirement for reproductive success. In a way, then, territorial behavior has the effect of allocating breeding space and limiting population size to that which the ecosystem can support. This kind of behavior is widespread in the animal kingdom and can be seen in such diverse groups as insects, spiders, fish, reptiles, birds, and mammals.

A Human beings are different from other animals, but only in the degree to which we employ different kinds of behavior. Read the following animals' behaviors and label them as either *imprinting, association, habituation,* or *insight.*

1. _____: A dog hears the sound of a can being opened. It runs into the kitchen and looks in its food dish.

2. _____: A chimpanzee uses a stick to knock a bunch of bananas off a tree.

3. _____: A newborn foal (a baby horse) follows its mother wherever she goes.

B Answer the following questions in complete sentences.

1. What is an example of associative learning from your own experience? Explain why you consider this behavior associative learning.

2. Why might imprinting be an uncommon form of learning for human beings? Explain your reasons for your answer.

3. What are some reasons why territorial behavior might be a disadvantage to an individual organism but a benefit to the species as a whole?

C On a separate piece of paper, create a chart or diagram to illustrate the information in the reading. Provide a title for your chart or diagram.

Writing about Figures

Examine the figures below. Write a paragraph in which you describe the types of behavior exhibited by the horses in each photograph. A vocabulary list has been provided. Choose words you need from the list.

associative learning	exploit	insight	resource allocation
component	hereditary	instinct	territorial behavior
dominance hierarchy	imprinting	reflexes	vertebrates
ecological niche	innate	relationship	

Wild stallions fighting

Horse act at the Moscow Circus

Name: _____ Date: _____

CHAPTER THREE TEST

Vocabulary

Complete the passage below with words from the following list. Use each word only once. You will not use all the words.

active	cultural	habitat	taboo
artifacts	expressed	passive	transmitted
concept	feature	stimuli	variable

The Concept of Culture

Perhaps the easiest characteristic of a cultural behavior to see is that culture is *learned*. The ants clearly didn't learn how to build nests, even as complex as that behavior might be. Rather, the behavior is built into their genes and is (1) _____ by a complex series of (2) _____ that elicit a complex set of responses. My accomplishment, on the other hand, was only possible through learning, and the skills and information I learned were in turn learned by those who instructed me, who learned it from someone else, and so on.

Learning used to be considered the only distinguishing (3) _____ between cultural and noncultural behaviors, but a moment's reflection will tell you that learning is not enough. Other creatures learn. My dogs, for example, have learned many things, including, of course, the (4) _____ (prohibition) against eliminating in the house, but these things would not really be considered (5) _____. Why not? What other differences are there?

A second characteristic of culture is that it involves *concepts, generalizations, abstractions,* and *ideas*. The ants are locked into the specifics of their nest-building behavior. It must work the same all the time. If some important (6) _____ is different, the ants cannot make specific adjustments. They don't, in other words, know what they are doing. Their behavior is not part of some larger (7) _____.

10 Tests © 2005 by Lorraine C. Smith. Duplication for classroom use is permitted.

There is another dimension to learning that is important. Learning in most organisms is (8) _____. They learn from imitation or from trial and error. For many birds, for example, singing just the right song is impossible unless they've heard another bird sing it. Singing itself is genetic, but the song must be learned. But learning can also be (9) _____, when information is *shared* among organisms, when it is (10) _____ from one organism to another extragenetically, that is, without any direct genetic influence, as in the birdsong example. The ants' basic information about nest-building is solely genetic. The information I acquired about wall-building was shared extragenetically.

Reading Comprehension

Read the passage below. As you read, highlight the important ideas and vocabulary used to express those ideas. Annotate the text. Then do the test exercises that follow.

Religious Beliefs as Part of a Culture's World View

We can open a window onto another group's world view by looking at their religious beliefs. Religion is not the same as world view. Religion is one aspect of a cultural system. But one function of religion in all societies is to allow people to **codify** their world view—to talk about, share, and pass on those assumptions about the way things are. Let's compare two rather distinct world views—that of Arctic peoples with those of certain societies from Southwest Asia (also called the Near East or Middle East) around 10,000 years ago.

The environment of peoples of the American Arctic (whom we may collectively refer to as Eskimo, although there is some disagreement over that usage) is one of the harshest environments of any human group. The Arctic never has been an easy place to live, and the Eskimo saw that world as one over which their control was limited, tenuous, and unstable.

How is this view reflected in Eskimo religion? In other words, how did the Eskimo codify this world view? There are many different Arctic peoples, both in North America and Asia, and so there are many specific individual cultural systems. We may look at a few aspects of one and, because there are certain similarities among peoples of this region, it can represent some generalizations about them all.

The Netsilik people live in the Hudson Bay region of Canada. Their name means "people of the seal" because seal hunting in the winter is a major focus of their lives, although they also hunt caribou and fish for salmon in the spring, summer, and fall. The Netsilik express their view of the world by believing that the natural world is under the control of the spirit world, and important natural phenomena—as well as all humans and animals—have spirits or souls. We say technically that the Netsilik, like many hunting peoples, are **polytheistic**—they recognize multiple supernatural beings.

The control of these souls over the physical world helps explain why things are as they are, especially why things can go wrong. Souls that have been wronged can cause misfortunes and thus there are many rules about how they should be treated. A newly killed seal, for instance, must be placed on fresh snow rather than the dirty floor of the igloo. The hunters beg the forgiveness of the spirit. Water is poured in the dead seal's mouth because its soul is still thirsty. Caribou souls are especially sensitive and no work on caribou hides can be done in sight of living caribou. If they see and are offended, their soul will not allow them to be caught. By adhering to these taboos the Netsilik gained at least some sense of influence over their difficult lives. Thus, not only the technology of the Netsilik but more abstract aspects of their culture can be linked to their interpretation of and response to the real world in which they live.

Contrast this with a second example. In Southwest Asia about 10,000 years ago, a major cultural event began to take place—the invention of farming. People with this cultural ability had direct control over the most important natural resource, food. Think of how that cultural change would eventually alter the world a people lived in and change their feelings about that world and their place in it. As the long history of farming influenced the physical and cultural worlds of this area, we see a change in world view reflected in three important religious traditions that originated in Southwest Asia—Judaism, Christianity, and Islam.

All three of these religions are **monotheistic**, that is, they recognize one supreme supernatural being. That one being, whom we can refer to as God in all three cases, brought about and has control over all natural phenomena, including human affairs. But in the Judeo-Christian-Islamic tradition, humans may petition God through prayer and action. They can ask God for favors. Humans have some sense of personal control in their dealings with the supernatural, even with an all-powerful being.

This is a clear reflection and articulation of a world view in which people are coming to see themselves as having a real ability to know and understand the world around them and to use that knowledge to exercise real control over their world for their own benefit. As people begin to view the world as clearly divided into the human and the natural, so too is there a division between humans and a single, omnipotent supernatural entity.

A Circle the correct answers.

1. What can we infer about the usage of the term *Eskimo* to describe the peoples of the American Arctic?
    a. The term is not acceptable to some people.
    b. The term is incorrect.
    c. The term is collective.

2. When the Netsilik have killed a seal, why do they put the seal's body on clean snow?
    a. because they do not want the seal meat to become dirty
    b. because they want to preserve the meat on the cold snow
    c. because they do not want the seal's soul to become evil

3. What might happen if the Netsilik work on a killed caribou where other caribou can see them?
    a. The caribou might attack the Netsilik for killing one of their species.
    b. The caribou's souls might keep them from being killed in the future.
    c. The caribou might run far away and become harder to hunt.

4. What did people in Southwest Asia 10,000 years ago have that the Netsilik people do not have?
    a. the ability to hunt wild animals
    b. belief in the supernatural
    c. control over obtaining food

B **Answer the following questions in complete sentences.**

1. How does a cultural group codify its world view?

2. Why do the Netsilik take such care with the bodies of the animals they kill?

3. How did the invention of farming initiate a change in world view among the people in Southwest Asia?

4. Under what general condition do people tend to move from polytheistic beliefs to monotheistic beliefs?

C **On a separate piece of paper, create a chart, flow chart, or diagram to illustrate the information in the reading. Provide a title for your chart, flow chart, or diagram.**

Writing about Figures

Examine the figures below. Write a paragraph in which you describe why the behaviors illustrated in the figures represent cultural or noncultural behavior. A vocabulary list has been provided. Choose words you need from the list.

artifact	cultural	generalization	realization
characteristic	extragenetic	noncultural	transmit
concept	feature	passive	variation

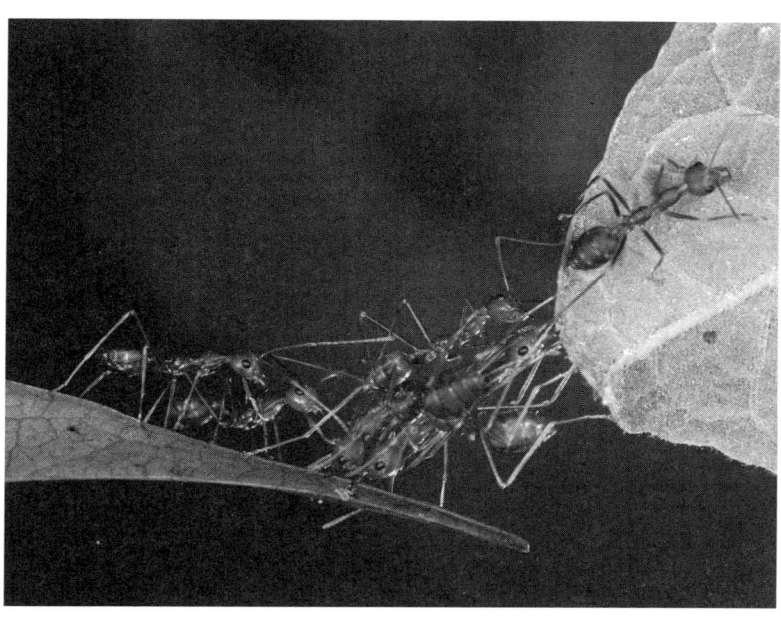

Weaver ants pulling two leaves together

Man learning to use a power saw

Name: _____ Date: _____

CHAPTER FOUR TEST

Vocabulary

Complete the passage below with words from the following list. Use each word only once. You will not use all the words.

acculturation	interact	phenomena	trait
applies	intervenes	polytheism	variation
expression	monotheistic	supernatural	world view

Making the World View Real

Beliefs are important, because beliefs are a direct reflection of our world view, our set of assumptions, attitudes, and responses that give rise to and hold together the cultural fabric of our lives. Except for personal survival, nothing is more important or more central to our existence. Religions are our way of making our (1) _____ real. They provide us with a means for communicating our assumptions about the world. They give us a medium for formulating values of behavior that correspond to the world view.

Religions vary greatly from society to society but the one (2) _____ they all have in common is the supernatural. **Religion** is a set of beliefs and behaviors pertaining to the supernatural. By *supernatural* we mean something—a force or power of being—that is outside the known laws of nature. Thus, one difference among societies is in which phenomena are dealt with by religion—a belief system—and which are dealt with using scientific knowledge.

Let's look at the ways in which religious (3) _____ differs among cultures. Like any cultural expression, religion varies in how it is geared to individual culture systems and in how it changes to keep pace with them. There are, of course, as many specific religious systems as there are cultures, but we can get an overview by noting the (4) _____ in some general aspects of religion.

In Chapter 3, we discussed the distinction between monotheistic and polytheistic religions and the connection between these and some general types of world view. (5) _____ tends to be found in societies like the Eskimo, that (6) _____ with their environments on a more personal level, where the people see themselves as one of many natural phenomena. Groups practicing polytheism tend not to have political systems with formal leadership. The supernatural reflects the natural in terms of social organization as well. (7) _____ systems are found in groups that have gained distinct control over their habitats—groups like the early agriculturalists of Southwest Asia. Such groups tend to have a hierarchical political system with formal leadership and full-time labor specialists.

16 Tests   © 2005 by Lorraine C. Smith. Duplication for classroom use is permitted.

Also showing variation is the degree to which the supernatural (8) _____ in the daily affairs of people. Generally, the more important scientific knowledge is to a people, the less direct is the influence of the gods. Natural (9) _____, including human actions, are attributed to natural forces. The degree and kind of intervention may also be related to the complexity of the social order. Especially where there are inequalities in wealth and power, rules for human behavior that are said to come directly from the (10) _____ may help to maintain the existing order (and, thus, the wealth and power of those who have it).

Reading Comprehension

Read the passage below. As you read, highlight the important ideas and vocabulary used to express those ideas. Annotate the text. Then do the test exercises that follow.

The Processes of Culture Change

Every cultural alteration—every new idea or new artifact—must start somewhere. Thus, at the base of all culture change are the related processes of **discovery** and **invention**. Discovery is the realization and understanding of some set of relationships—anything from the nature of fire to the reaction of the people of a society to some aspect of their environment. Invention refers to the creation of artifacts, whether concrete (tools) or abstract (institutions), that put the discovery to use. Discovery is knowledge; invention is application.

It is important to understand that, once adopted, a new discovery and its initial applications become part of a cultural system, where their presence brings about changes in the system. Think about such things as the domestication of the horse, the invention of wheeled vehicles, and more recent innovations such as the production and harnessing of electricity the understanding of the energy within the atom.

Each society can only discover and invent so much. Thus, the second basic process of culture change is the **diffusion** of discoveries and artifacts, i.e., the giving and taking of culture among different societies. This is thought to be responsible, on average, for 90 percent of a society's cultural inventory. Though we are, by our very nature, an inventive, creative species, we nonetheless rely heavily on borrowed items for stimulating and bringing about change. Societies isolated from outside contact change slowly. Those with greater opportunity for contact—and thus for borrowing—change more rapidly. This emphasis on diffusion is sometimes hard to grasp because once an item is borrowed it is modified and adapted to the borrowing culture and becomes a part of its cultural system. It becomes so firmly a part of that system that we don't think about the fact that it may not have originated within that culture.

There are two other basic recognized processes of culture change that are, in a sense, extreme forms of invention and diffusion. One is **acculturation**, defined as rapid diffusion under the influence of a dominant society. This may occur voluntarily or by force and with violence. Examples of the latter are all too common. Native Americans, for instance, were quickly acculturated into the European-based society of the colonial powers and later the United States. As just one example, many Indians in the American Southwest still practice Catholicism and have Spanish surnames, a remnant of several hundred years of Spanish presence in the region. Countries conquered during war are forced to take on at least some of the cultural aspects of their conquerors, although the conquerors can also be influenced by the cultures they defeat. For example, when the European Christians conquered and ruled Islamic Spain, from the eleventh through the fifteenth centuries, they found a wealth of written knowledge in science, mathematics, and philosophy, some of it passed down from classical Greece. This knowledge then entered and had a profound effect on Western Europe's history.

Another process of culture change is **revolution**. Usually thought of in the context of violent overthrow of an existing government—as in the American, French, and Russian revolutions—a revolution can also refer to a radical change in other aspects of society. There are scientific revolutions. The discoveries of Copernicus, Darwin, and Einstein come to mind—discoveries that radically and fairly rapidly changed the very way we think. A revolution in the sense of a process of culture change can, I believe, be thought of as rapid invention—new ideas and applications from within a society (or borrowed and radically adapted from outside) that thoroughly alter that society.

These are the processes that bring about changes in cultures. All these processes should not be thought of as independent and separate, of course. They can work together in interaction. For example, the stimulus for an invention can diffuse from another culture, even if the invention itself does not. This, in fact, is known as *stimulus diffusion*.

A Match each term with its definition.

1. ____ acculturation
2. ____ diffusion
3. ____ discovery
4. ____ invention
5. ____ revolution

a. the process by which new understandings are gained through new connections of ideas or natural phenomena

b. the process by which some characteristic of a culture experiences a sudden or dramatic change

c. the process by which a culture changes through the exchange of artifacts among different cultures

d. the process by which a more powerful culture influences another culture to change very quickly through cultural exchange

e. the process by which new ideas or creations are put to practical use

B Answer each question in complete sentences.

1. The author states that the processes of discovery and invention are related in the sense that discovery is knowledge and invention is the application of that knowledge. Might it be possible to have one without the other? Explain your reasons for your answer.

_____
_____
_____

2. The diffusion of discoveries and artifacts leads to culture change in societies that are in contact with other societies. What might be some of the disadvantages of this process of culture change?

_____
_____
_____

3. Can the invention of the automobile be considered a revolution in terms of culture change? Explain your reasons for your answer.

_____
_____
_____

C On a separate piece of paper, create a chart, flow chart, or diagram to illustrate the information in the reading. Provide a title for your chart, flow chart, or diagram.

Writing about Figures

Examine the figures below. Write a paragraph in which you describe the type of culture change represented by the telescope and by the Cherokee alphabet. A vocabulary list has been provided. Choose words you need from the list.

acculturation	cultural system	intentionally	stimulus diffusion
alter	diffusion	interact	syncretism
application	discovery	invention	trait
contact	influence	revolution	variation

Telescope and lens of Galileo Galilei

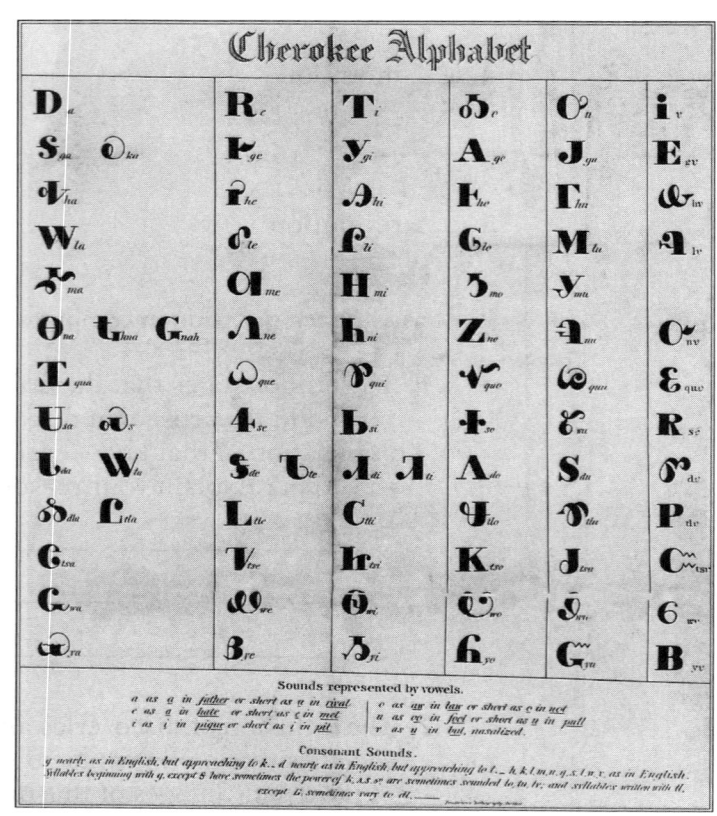

Sequoyah's Cherokee alphabet

Name: _____ Date: _____

CHAPTER FIVE TEST

Vocabulary

Complete the passage below with words from the following list. Use each word only once. You will not use all the words.

advancement	contradictions	Galileo	revolved
Aristotle	doctrine	observation	scholarship
astonishing	experimentation	perplexing	systematized

The Aristotelian Origins of Western Scientific Beliefs

Scholarly activity ceased in most of Europe through the Dark Ages, and the works of Aristotle were forgotten. (1) _____ continued in the Byzantine and Islamic empires, and various texts of Aristotle's teachings were reintroduced to Europe during the eleventh and twelfth centuries and translated into Latin. The Church, at that time the dominant political and cultural force in Western Europe, first prohibited the works of Aristotle and then accepted and incorporated them into Christian (2) _____. Any attack on Aristotle was an attack on the Church itself. It was in this climate that Galileo effectively challenged Aristotle's ideas on motion, and ushered in a new method of knowing—experimentation.

One of the most astonishing yet perplexing moments in the history of Western thought is the emergence of the new science (in the seventeenth century). It was (3) _____ because it seemed truly new. The discoveries of the stargazers, like those of the sea explorers, challenged people's most basic assumptions and beliefs. Men dropping balls from towers or peering at the skies though a glass claimed that they had disproved thousands of years of certainty about the nature of the universe. But the new science was (4) _____ because it seemed to loosen the moorings of everything that educated people thought they knew about their world. Nothing could be more disorienting than to challenge common sense. People needed to do little more than wake up in the morning to know that the Sun moved from east to west while the Earth stood still. But mathematics, (5) _____, and deduction were needed to understand that the Earth was in constant motion and that it (6) _____ around the Sun.

The scientific revolution was the opening of a new era in European history. After two centuries of classical revival, European thinkers had finally come against the limits of ancient knowledge. Ancient wisdom had served Europeans well, and it was not to be discarded lightly. But one by one, the certainties of the past were being called into question. The explanations of the universe and the natural world that had been advanced by (7) _____ and codified by his followers no longer seemed adequate. There were too many (8) _____ between theory and (9) _____, too many things that did not fit. Yet breaking the hold of Aristotelianism was no easy task. A full century was to pass before even learned people would accept the proofs that the Earth revolved around the Sun. Even then, the most famous of them—(10) _____—had to recant those views or be condemned as a heretic.

Reading Comprehension

Read the passage below. As you read, highlight the important ideas and vocabulary used to express those ideas. Annotate the text. Then do the test exercises that follow.

The Seventeenth-Century Scientific Revolution

The two essential characteristics of the new science were that it was materialistic and mathematical. Its materialism was contained in the realization that the universe is composed of matter in motion. That meant that the stars and planets were not made of some perfect ethereal (abstract) substance but of the same matter that was found on earth. They were thus subject to the same rules of motion as were earthly objects. The mathematics of the new science was contained in the realization that calculation had to replace common sense as the basis for understanding the universe. More importantly, scientific experimentation took the form of measuring repeatable phenomena. When Galileo attempted to develop a theory of acceleration, he rolled a brass ball down an inclined plane and recorded the time and distance of its descent 100 times before he was satisfied with his results.

There was much to be said for Aristotle's understanding of the world, for his cosmology. For one thing, it was harmonious. It incorporated a view of the physical world that coincided with a view of the spiritual and moral one. The heavens were unchangeable, and therefore they were better than the earth. The sun, moon, and planets were all faultless spheres, unblemished and immune from decay. Their motion was circular because the circle was the perfect form of motion. The earth was at the center of the universe because it was the heaviest planet and because it was at the center of the Great Chain of Being, between the underworld of spirits and the upper world of gods. The second advantage to the Aristotelian world view was that it was easily incorporated into Christianity. Aristotle's description of the heavens as being composed of a closed system of crystalline rings that held the sun, moon, and planets in their circular orbits around the earth left room for God and the angels to reside just beyond the last ring.

There were, of course, problems with Aristotle's explanation of the universe. For one thing, if the sun revolved in a perfect circle around the earth, then why were the seasons not perfectly equal? If the planets all revolved around the earth in circles, then why did they look nearer or farther, brighter or darker at different times of year? To solve those problems, a lot of ingenious hypotheses were advanced.

In the 1490s, Nicolaus Copernicus (1473–1543) came to the Polish University of Krakow, which had one of the leading mathematical faculties in Europe. There they taught the latest astronomical theories and vigorously debated the existence of eccentric circles and epicycles. Copernicus came to Krakow for a liberal arts education before pursuing a degree in Church law. He became fascinated by astronomy and puzzled by the debate over planetary motion. Copernicus believed, like Aristotle, that the simplest explanations were the best. If the sun was at the center of the universe and the earth simply another planet in orbit, then many of the most elaborate explanations of planetary motion were unnecessary. "At rest, in the middle of everything is the Sun," Copernicus wrote in *On the Revolutions of the Heavenly Spheres* (1543). "For in this most beautiful temple who would place this lamp in another or better position than that from which it can light up the whole thing at the same time?" Because Copernicus accepted most of the rest of the traditional Aristotelian explanation, especially the belief that the planets moved in circles, his sun-centered universe was only slightly better at predicting the position of the planets than the traditional earth-centered one, but Copernicus's idea stimulated other astronomers to make new calculations.

A Circle the correct answers.

1. Why is the realization that the universe is made of matter in motion so critical to the new science?

    a. because it helped to separate the new science from religion

    b. because it enabled Galileo to perform experiments on acceleration

    c. because it enabled scientists to create universal laws of motion

2. Why was Aristotle probably sure his hypotheses were correct?

    a. because his theories were based on common sense

    b. because he conducted careful experiments to prove them

    c. because the simplest explanations are never wrong

3. How did Copernicus's sun-centered hypothesis revolutionize science?

    a. It contradicted the Church's views on the nature of the universe.

    b. It greatly simplified ideas about planetary motion.

    c. It enabled people to accurately predict the planets' positions.

B Answer the following questions in complete sentences.

1. In scientific experimentation, why is it essential to repeat the same experiment many times?

2. How did Galileo's theorizing about the nature of acceleration differ from Aristotle's theorizing about the nature of the universe?

3. What was the Copernicus's biggest contribution to the Scientific Revolution? Explain your reason for your answer.

C On a separate piece of paper, create a chart, flow chart, diagram, or outline to illustrate the information in the reading. Provide a title for your chart, flow chart, diagram, or outline.

Writing about Figures

Examine the figure below. Write a paragraph in which you describe what is taking place. A vocabulary list has been provided. Choose words you need from the list.

academic	Aristotle	experimentation	observation
acceleration	astronomy	Galileo Galilei	scholarship
aim	contradiction	hypothesis	systematize

'They were seen to fall evenly.'
28

Galileo dropping two balls of different sizes from the Tower of Pisa

CHAPTER SIX TEST

Vocabulary

Complete the passage below with words from the following list. Use each word only once. You will not use all the words.

celestial	enumerate	observation	scientific revolution
credence	hemisphere	orbits	telescope
debate	instrument	prominences	terrestrial

Galileo Galilei's Astronomical Observations

No single individual is as much associated with the (1) _____ as Galileo Galilei. He made formative contributions to mathematics, physics, and astronomy, but he also served as a lightning rod for the dissemination of the newest ideas. He popularized the work of Copernicus. Among his many accomplishments, Galileo was the first to use a(n) (2) _____ to make scientific observations.

About ten months ago a report reached my ears that a certain Fleming had constructed a spyglass by means of which visible objects, though very distant from the eye of the observer, were distinctly seen as if nearby. Of this truly remarkable effect several experiences were related, to which some persons gave (3) _____ while others denied them. A few days later the report was confirmed to me in a letter from a noble Frenchman at Paris, Jacques Badovere, which caused me to apply myself wholeheartedly to inquire into the means by which I might arrive at the invention of a similar instrument. This I did shortly afterwards, my basis being the theory of refraction. . . . Sparing neither labor nor expense, I succeeded in constructing for myself so excellent a(n) (4) _____ that objects seen by means of it appeared nearly one thousand times larger and over thirty times closer than when regarded with our natural vision.

It would be superfluous to (5) _____ the number and importance of the advantages of such an instrument at sea as well as on land. But forsaking (6) _____ observations, I turned to (7) _____ ones, and first I saw the moon from as near at hand as if it were scarcely two terrestrial radii.

. . . . *Let us speak first of that surface of the moon which faces us. For greater clarity I distinguish two parts of this surface, a lighter and a darker; the lighter part seems to surround and to pervade the whole* (8) _____*, while the darker part discolors the moon's surface like a kind of cloud, and makes it appear covered with spots. . . . From* (9) _____ *of these spots repeated many times I have been led to the opinion and conviction that the surface of the moon is not smooth, uniform, and precisely spherical as a great number of philosophers believe it (and the other heavenly bodies) to be, but is uneven, rough, and full of cavities and* (10) _____*, being not unlike the face of the earth, relieved by chains of mountains and deep valleys.*

Reading Comprehension

Read the passage below. As you read, highlight the important ideas and vocabulary used to express those ideas. Annotate the text. Then do the test exercises that follow.

The New Science and the New Scientists

In Chapter 5, we read about Copernicus and his description of a sun-centered (i.e., heliocentric) universe. Although he placed the sun in the center of the universe, with the Earth and planets revolving around it, he maintained that they all orbited the sun in perfectly circular orbits. He also did not challenge other Aristotelian teachings. This challenge was left for others to make, based on their observations, mathematical calculations, and logical deductions. These people included Tycho Brahe, Johannes Kepler, Galileo Galilei, and Isaac Newton.

Under the patronage of the king of Denmark, Tycho Brahe (1546–1601) built a large observatory to study planetary motion. In 1572, Brahe discovered a nova, a brightly burning star that was previously unknown. The discovery challenged the idea of an immutable, or unchanging, universe composed of crystalline rings. In 1577, the appearance of a comet cutting through the supposedly impenetrable rings punched another hole into the old cosmology.

Brahe's own views were a hybrid of old and new. He believed that all planets but the earth revolved around the sun and that the sun and the planets revolved around a fixed earth. To demonstrate his theory, Brahe and his students compiled the largest and most accurate mathematical tables of planetary motion yet known. From this research, Brahe's pupil Johannes Kepler (1571–1630), one of the great mathematicians of the age, formulated laws of planetary motion. Kepler discovered that planets orbited the sun in an elliptical rather than a circular path, which accounted for their movements nearer and farther from the earth. More importantly, he demonstrated that there was a precise mathematical relationship between the speed with which a planet revolved and its distance from the sun. Kepler's findings supported the view that the galaxy was heliocentric and that the heavens, like the earth, were made of matter that was subject to physical laws.

What Kepler demonstrated mathematically, the Italian astronomer Galileo Galilei (1564–1642) confirmed by observation. Creating a telescope by using magnifying lenses and a long tube, Galileo saw parts of the heavens that had never been dreamed of before. In 1610, he discovered four moons of Jupiter, proving conclusively that all heavenly bodies did not revolve around the earth. He observed the landscape of the earth's moon and described it as full of mountains, valleys, and rivers. It was of the same imperfect form as the earth itself. He even found spots on the sun, which suggested that it, too, was composed of ordinary matter. Through the telescope, Galileo gazed upon an unimaginable universe. "The Galaxy is nothing else but a mass of innumerable stars," he wrote. Galileo's greatest scientific discoveries had to do with motion—he was the first to posit a law of inertia—but his greatest contribution to the new science was his popularization of the Copernican theory. He took the debate over the structure of the universe to the public, popularizing the discoveries of scientists in his vigorous Italian tracts.

As news of his experiments and discoveries spread, Galileo became famous throughout the Continent, and his support for heliocentrism became a celebrated cause. In 1616, the Roman Catholic church cautioned him against promoting his views. In 1633, a year after publishing his *A Dialogue Between the Two Great Systems of the World*, Galileo was tried by the Inquisition for heresy and forced specifically to recant the idea that the earth moves. He spent the rest of his life under house arrest. Galileo insisted that there was nothing in the new science that was anti-Christian. He rejected the view that his discoveries refuted the Bible, arguing that the words of the Bible were often difficult to interpret and that nature was another way in which God revealed himself. In fact, Galileo feared that the Church's opposition to what he deemed as scientific truth could only bring the Church into disrepute.

The greatest of all English scientists was the mathematician and physicist Sir Isaac Newton (1642–1727). He made stunning contributions to the sciences of optics, physics, astronomy, and mathematics, and his magnum opus, *Mathematical Principles of Natural Philosophy* (1687), is one of a handful of the most important scientific works ever composed. Most important, Newton solved the single most perplexing problem: If the world was composed of matter in motion, what was motion?

Newton came from a moderately prosperous background and was trained at a local grammar school before entering Cambridge University. There was little in his background or education to suggest his unique talents, and in fact his most important discoveries were not appreciated until years after he had made them. Newton was the first to understand the composition of light, the first to develop a calculus, and the first to build a reflecting telescope. Newton became a professor at Cambridge, but he spent much of his time alone.

Although Galileo had developed a *theory of inertia*, the idea that a body at rest stays at rest, most materialists believed that motion was the result of the interaction of objects and that it could be calculated mathematically. From his experiments, Newton formulated the concept of force and his famous laws of motion: (1) that objects at rest or in uniform linear motion remain in such a state unless acted upon by an external force; (2) that changes in motion are proportional to force; (3) that for every action there is an equal and opposite reaction. From the laws of motion, Newton advanced one step further. If the world was no more than matter in motion and if all motion was subject to the same laws, then the movement of the planets could be explained in the same way as the movement of an apple falling from a tree. There was a mathematical relationship between attraction and repulsion—a universal gravitation, as Newton called it—that governed the movement of all objects. Newton's theory of gravity joined together Kepler's astronomy and Galileo's physics. The mathematical, materialistic world of the new science was now complete.

A Circle the correct answers.

1. Why did the appearance of a comet in 1577 help to disprove Aristotle's beliefs?

   a. because the comet did not revolve around the earth

   b. because the comet was not immutable

   c. because the comet went through the crystalline rings

2. Which diagram illustrates Brahe's view of the universe?
(E = Earth; S = sun; P = planet)

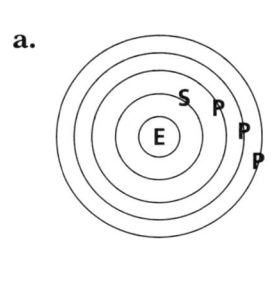

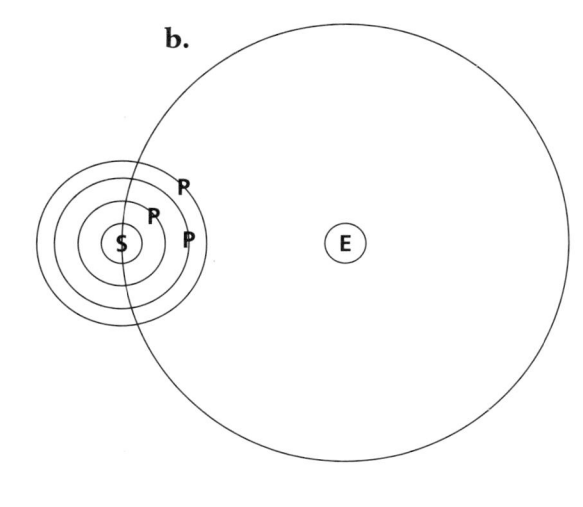

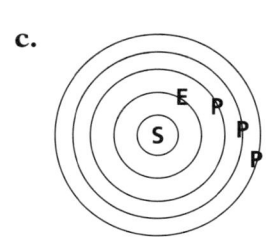

3. What was the understanding behind Newton's laws of motion?

   a. All objects throughout the universe obey the same laws of motion.

   b. All heavenly objects such as the sun and the planets obey the same laws of motion.

   c. All objects on the Earth obey the same laws of motion. All heavenly objects obey different laws of motion.

B Answer the following questions in complete sentences.

1. How did Galileo's discovery of four moons of Jupiter disprove Aristotle's earth-centered view of the universe?

   _____
   _____
   _____

2. How did Galileo explain his science in terms of what was written in the Bible?

   _____
   _____
   _____

3. Why was Newton's concept of universal gravitation so important to science?

   _____
   _____
   _____

C On a separate piece of paper, create a chart, flow chart, diagram, or outline to illustrate the information in the reading. Provide a title for your chart, flow chart, diagram, or outline.

Writing about Figures

Examine the figure below. Write a paragraph in which you describe what is in the photograph, explain how it supported Galileo's beliefs, and identify the consequences to Galileo when he published his findings. A vocabulary list has been provided. Choose words you need from the list.

celestial	heliocentric	instrument	orbit
debate	heresy	interpret	recant
deny	immutable	laws of motion	telescope
dissemination	impenetrable	observation	terrestrial

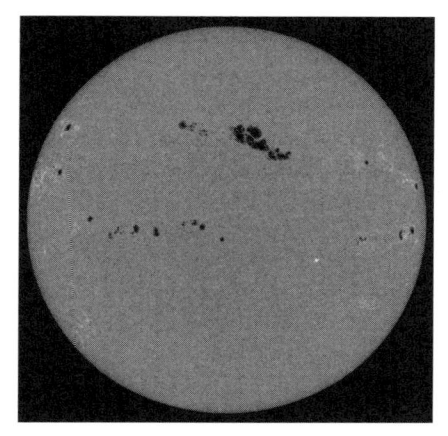

The sun's sunspots

Name: _____ Date: _____

CHAPTER SEVEN TEST

Vocabulary

Complete the passage below with words from the following list. Use each word only once. You will not use all the words.

antiquity	illusory	inspiration	perspective
artists	impetus	Middle Ages	Renaissance
converging	incorporating	models	representations

Art and Artists in History

The traditional classification of the Western visual arts as manual, or mechanical, arts was transformed in the fourteenth and fifteenth centuries. Both (1) _____ and writers began to emphasize the scientific and intellectual aspects of art, often (2) _____ the liberal arts into the education of artists. It was argued that mathematics, for example, was necessary for the study of proportion, and that geometry figured in the calculation of (3) _____. The artist was beginning to be seen as an educated professional versed in both the practice and the theory of art. This attitude that the artist had to be a skilled and educated individual was accompanied by a new social status: artists became the companions of intellectuals, princes, popes, and emperors.

Naturalistic (4) _____ of human figures were introduced to Western art in the Hellenistic and ancient Roman periods, a period often referred to as (5) _____. These attitudes toward the figure in art, reintroduced in fifteenth-century Italy, helped to establish the foundation for the cultural epoch known as the (6) _____, French for "rebirth" (circa 1400–1620 C.E.). The reasons behind the appeal of antiquity in this period are not easy to simplify, but the richness and splendor of antique monuments, even in ruins, had had an impact throughout the (7) _____, and as society and economic life blossomed at the end of the medieval period, such monuments provided appropriate (8) _____ for new construction. The new self-confidence expressed in politics, business, and learning in the fifteenth century found important models and (9) _____ not only in ancient texts but also in ancient sculpture, especially the Greek emphasis on the dignity and beauty of the human figure and the Roman ability to capture the individual in portraiture.

For Italian Renaissance artists, the models of classical antiquity provided a(n) (10) _____ for artistic transformation, but it would be a mistake to view these artists as merely copying ancient works of art. They adapted the classical aesthetic to the attitudes of their own times, creating works of art distinctly different from those of antiquity.

Reading Comprehension

Read the passage below. As you read, highlight the important ideas and vocabulary used to express those ideas. Annotate the text. Then do the test exercises that follow.

The Early Renaissance in Italy and Flanders

The Renaissance concept of humanism had a profound philosophical foundation. The title *humanist* was originally applied to a teacher of humanistic studies, a curriculum that included rhetoric, grammar, poetry, history, and moral philosophy; at the base of many of these disciplines was the study of ancient texts on these topics in Latin and eventually, in Greek as well. Already in the fourteenth century, scholars and writers had been inspired by the ideas they found in ancient Greek and Roman texts, which formed their new intellectual and scientific interest in understanding the world. The praise for the deeds of great figures from antiquity that the humanists found in the Greek and Roman texts supported the notions of pride and fame that were becoming important in a society whose major figures were successful businessmen and bankers.

The dignity of the individual and the new self-consciousness promoted by the humanists had an important influence on attitudes about artists. In contrast to the prevalent medieval attitude that the artist was a humble craftsperson serving God, some Renaissance artists were viewed as trained intellectuals, versed in the classics and geometry. Artists became famous; in 1481, for example, an author named Cristoforo Landino made a list of Italian and Flemish artists and praised them for their skill and innovations. Artists began to sign their works with more frequency, and one artist, Lorenzo Ghiberti, wrote his autobiography. The modern ideal of the artist as a genius has its origins in these developments in the fifteenth century.

During the fifteenth century, artists and workshops received a variety of secular and religious commissions. Rulers continued to employ works of art for the traditional purposes of exalting and consolidating their power, but now their imagery more often had an ancient basis and/or was inspired by models from antiquity. A relatively new development is patronage by city governments in the Italian communes and patronage by the mercantile class in Flanders and Italy; based on the writing of the humanists, patronage was now viewed as an important activity of the responsible and enlightened citizen. While devotional images were produced in increasing numbers to adorn the rooms of the expanding middle class, new types of art—portraits, mythological subjects, and secular decorations—were commissioned by individuals to adorn their private palaces, town houses, or country villas.

The study of perspective, the rendering of figures or objects in illusionary space, was an important innovation in Renaissance art. Perspective had been a conscious development in ancient Greek painting, and many examples of Roman art attest to the accomplished use of perspective in antiquity. During the Middle Ages, however, pictorial reproduction of the physical world became less significant within a culture that emphasized spiritual and otherworldly values. Perspective gradually became valued in the later Middle Ages, but a coherent system allowing artists to determine the relative diminution of size of figures and objects was lacking.

That problem was solved by Filippo Brunelleschi (1377–1446), the Early Renaissance architect. Around 1415, Brunelleschi demonstrated a **scientific perspective** (also called **linear** and **vanishing-point perspective**) system in two lost paintings. Scientific perspective is based on the assumption that parallel lines receding from us seem to converge at a point on the horizon. This is the basis for the meeting of these lines at the vanishing point. Brunelleschi's new perspective system was incorporated in works by other artists, including Masaccio in *The Trinity with the Virgin Mary, Saint John, and Two Donors* and Perugino in *Christ Giving the Keys to Saint Peter*. In this work, the diagonal lines created by the recession of architectural elements parallel to each other converge at a vanishing point. Additionally, scientific perspective is combined with **atmospheric**

perspective for a unified effect that encompasses vast spaces, correctly proportioned figures, and the subtle qualities of the sky and distant landscape as they appear to the eye.

In Flanders, a prosperous new merchant society based on the wool trade and banking was established during the fourteenth and fifteenth centuries. Flanders was distinguished by a rich and diverse culture, which included a revolutionary school of composers that dominated European musical developments throughout the century. Northern intellectuals, however, were not very interested in the revival of the forms and subject matter of ancient Greece and Rome that were so important to the Italians.

FLEMISH PAINTING: THE LIMBOURG BROTHERS

The puff of frosty breath from the mouth of the figure hurrying across the farmyard and the smoke curling from the chimney are the kinds of subtle details that characterize the comprehensive realism developing in Flemish painting at the beginning of the fifteenth century. The traditional calendar page for February showed people sitting by a fire, but the Limbourg brothers' representation encompasses a modest farm, complete with dovecote, beehives, and sheepfold, set within a vast snowy landscape with a distant village. Several figures reveal the peasants' restricted winter activities. The sky is no longer merely a flat blue background, but offers atmospheric midwinter effects that reveal the Limbourgs' study of natural phenomena.

The *Très Riches Heures du Duc de Berry* marks a final phase in the development of manuscript painting in the North. This sumptuous manuscript, with 130 illustrations, includes devotions for different periods of the day in a format that is called a Book of Hours, thus the book's name. The heightened interest in representing naturalistic lighting effects, panoramic landscapes, and precise details explains why this manuscript has been so admired and its compositions so often copied by later artists.

A Match each term with its definition.

1. ____ atmospheric perspective

a. This is the point where lines that are not parallel come together to create a visual effect such that objects at different distances are correctly proportioned.

2. ____ commission

b. In a painting, usually of an outdoor scene, an artist creates a particular effect by ensuring that everything in the painting is shown exactly as a person would really see it.

3. ____ convergence

c. This term refers to the visual effect in a painting where objects that are close to the viewer are painted larger than objects that should be farther away from the viewer.

4. ____ natural phenomena

d. Someone pays an artist to create a particular work of art for his or her own home, or for placing somewhere else, such as a church.

5. ____ scientific perspective

e. These include everything around us, for example, rivers, mountains, animals, rain, and clouds.

B Answer the following questions in complete sentences.

1. In the early Renaissance, in what ways did people acknowledge the dignity of the individual and the new self-consciousness that humanists were promoting?

   _____

   _____

   _____

2. How did the new concept of humanism change the subjects artists chose or were commissioned to include in their work?

   _____

   _____

   _____

3. During the Renaissance, what was the main difference between Italian art and Flemish art?

   _____

   _____

   _____

C On a separate piece of paper, create a chart, flow chart, diagram, or outline to illustrate the information in the reading. Provide a title for your chart, flow chart, diagram, or outline.

Writing about Figures

Examine the figure below. Write a paragraph in which you describe and analyze the elements of the painting. A vocabulary list has been provided. Choose words you need from the list.

artist	converge	elevate	perspective
commission	diagonal lines	humanism	Renaissance
composition	diminution	illusionary	vanishing point perspective

Christ Giving the Keys to Saint Peter *by Perugino (1482)*

Name: _____ Date: _____

CHAPTER EIGHT TEST

Vocabulary

Complete the passage below with words from the following list. Use each word only once. You will not use all the words.

aesthetic	commissioned	nurtured	representing
calligraphy	composition	patronage	reverence
canons	depicted	realistic	Way of Nature

Art and Artists in China

Among cultures outside the Western tradition, China (1) _____ the oldest continuous painting tradition in the world. Its historical isolation, imperial (2) _____, art academies, and a bureaucratic elite of Confucian scholar-officials contributed to a unique tradition in the visual arts. Painters such as Ni Zan were part of the cultured elite who were the main participants in the Chinese classical tradition. Among the Chinese aristocracy, painting and (3) _____ were revered media for the preservation of social, political, and aesthetic values.

Chinese painting is derived from the art of writing and is, therefore, a linear art. Its brushwork is imbued with calligraphic formulas. The highest (4) _____ aim of the literati painters was to capture the spirit of what was (5) _____, rather than merely its appearance. For these literati painters, the creative process embodied the *dao*, or (6) _____, with its holistic vision of organic and metaphysical properties. In many Chinese paintings, idea and technique are one; the act of painting and the picture itself both carry meaning.

The earliest-known treatise (essay) on aesthetics was written in the second quarter of the sixth century by a man named Xie He (c. 500–c. 535). What made the treatise so influential was its Preface, known as the Six Canons of Painting, which were used to judge painters and paintings. The (7) _____ have been translated and interpreted many times. An approximate translation of the Six Canons is:

1. A painting must have spirit or breath of life (*qi yun*).
2. The brushwork must be structurally sound.
3. The painting must faithfully portray forms.
4. A painting must have fidelity of color.
5. A painting must also be a properly planned (8) _____.
6. A painting must transmit knowledge of past painting traditions.

The first canon, animation through spirit consonance, emphasizes the need for painting to have *qi yun*. **Qi** was thought to be the cosmic spirit that vitalized all things; to capture its essence was fundamental for "good" painting. Canons 2–5 clearly concentrate on technical matters, and canon 6 emphasizes the transmission of and (9) _____ for tradition. Xie He's treatise remained the backbone of aesthetic criticism until the modern period in China, when its imperial, elitist roots were challenged by new socialist policies.

The ideals of painting of the tenth century were written down by a contemporary of Li Cheng named Ching Hao, in his essay *Record of Brush Methods*, or *Essay on Landscape Painting*. This logical system first lays down the concept of painting and then its expression. It distinguishes further between resemblance, which reproduces the formal, outward aspects of what is depicted, and truth (or spirit), which involves knowing and representing inner reality. Correct balance between (10) _____ visible forms of nature and their deeper significance was the goal of these Chinese painters.

Reading Comprehension

Read the passage below. As you read, highlight the important ideas and vocabulary used to express those ideas. Annotate the text. Then do the test exercises that follow.

Chinese Art: Landscape Painting

Li Cheng (active from about 940 to 967) as a person was thought to represent the ideal Chinese painter—an artist who claimed descent from the imperial clan of the Tang dynasty (618–907), was educated in the humanities through study of the *Classic Books* (ancient texts on history, philosophy, and literature), and was occupied with painting for his own delight without ambition for honors or advancement. A scholar and a gentleman, he enjoyed a quiet life devoted to the philosophic study of Nature as opposed to merely copying forms in the out-of-doors (nature). **Monochrome** ink paintings of landscape were the preferred type of art produced by Li Cheng (such as *Buddhist Temple in the Hills after Rain*) and his colleagues.

Like many other landscape painters of the tenth century, Li Cheng had a preference for autumnal or wintry scenes full of bleak, stony crags, gnarled trees with leafless crab-claw-shaped branches, and looming distant peaks. He shares with other landscapists of the period a preference for monochrome ink, laid on the silk in broad and jagged strokes, to describe the essential outlines of the rocks, trees, and buildings. These shapes are then broken up and modeled with washes of ink. On top of the washes are placed **cun**, small brush strokes dabbed on quickly to create the sense of texture. Such paintings were then mounted on a vertical hanging or horizontal hand scroll. Closely associated with calligraphy, the brush paintings of China were produced for and by the intelligentsia, who painted as an avocation.

The Chinese doctrine of realism seen here aims for truth to natural appearance but not at the expense of a pictorial examination of how Nature operates. In Li Cheng's painting, the bent and twisted trees, for example, are organically constructed to expose their full skeletons—roots, trunk, branches, and even the dormant buds ready for spring awakening. This approach to realism also explains the attitude behind **shifting perspective** in Chinese painting. Shifting perspective allows for a journey and for a powerful personal impact on the individual participant. These paintings were meant to be visual exercises that allowed for examination of both the structure of nature or the universe and the contemplation of minute details. The power of these paintings is to take us out of ourselves and to provide spiritual solace and refreshment.

There was important support for landscape painters during the Five Dynasties (907–960) and the Northern Song dynasty (960–1126). An important occurrence of the period was the initial printing of the *Classical Texts* in 952; for the first time, books became inexpensive and abundant. Scholars multiplied, and the knowledge of ancient literature was more widespread. The prevailing pacifist policies and a series of enlightened sovereigns who were tolerant, humane, artistic, and intellectual provided substantial and consistent patronage for the arts. The Song period produced the first important academy of painting in the Far East; among the early members were the landscapists.

The Song dynasty was an age of many-sided intellectual activity—poetry, history, and especially, philosophy. Characteristic of Song thought was the return to older Chinese sources, a conscious archaism and cultural introspection. The renaissance of classical literature branched off into the formation of a new system of philosophy called neo-Confucianism, which enveloped traditional moral and ethical teachings with Daoist thinking about nature and the cosmos, especially as presented in the *I-jing* (*Book of Changes*). No distinction was made between the law of nature and moral law. The world was thought to be inspired by the "Supreme Ultimate" (or what the Daoists called the *dao*, or the Way); the neo-Confucianists referred to this as *li* (law), a moral law that was identical to the ethical code upon which human conduct should be modeled. These Song thinkers were also interested in correspondences in nature. The manifestation of *li* painting included faithfulness to nature as well as conventionalized symbols for representation of rocks, foliage, bark, water, and so forth. *Li* also governed the way a picture was put together.

Under pressure from the Jin Tartars on the northern borders of China, the Song court fled south in 1127. In 1135, a new capital was founded at Hangzhou, where the academy of painting was reestablished under imperial patronage and every effort was made to assemble an imperial art collection equal to that of the Northern Song emperors. The Southern Song rulers were even more concerned with internal affairs than their predecessors, and a new mode of painting evolved that focused on depiction of what was nearby and up close.

Later Southern Song landscape painters such as Xia Gui (active 1180–1230) concentrated on rivers, lakes, and mists of south China. Xia Gui developed a shorthand manner in which forms are suggested rather than depicted, as they had been in the earlier style of Li Cheng and Guo Xi. His softer and less literal expression is organized asymmetrically, in a style called a "one-corner" composition by the Chinese. There is more mist than ink, and the subjective expression omits large sections of the landscape to concentrate on closer components. Xia Gui evokes a mood; he does not describe a particular place. *Sailboat in the Rain* was commissioned by the imperial court. The inscription in the album leaf to the left of the painting is written by the Emperor Gaozong (1127–1162) of the Southern Song Dynasty, and is based on a poem written by Su Shi (1036–1101), a Northern Song poet. The Emperor changed some of the words in the original to suit his own mood:

> While sailing through endless rain,
> I enjoyed a good sleep.
> While boating all day long,
> We cut through the wind from the shore.

Xia Gui and other painters at court were associated with the politically weak and ineffectual court of the Southern Song in subsequent periods. For later Chinese critics, who commingled aesthetic and moral judgment, the South Song paintings were less highly valued than they were in Japan and the West.

A Circle the correct answers.

1. What did tenth-century Chinese landscape painters have in common?

    a. They were descended from imperial families.

    b. They liked to paint with monochrome ink.

    c. They painted to demonstrate shifting perspective.

2. What did the Five Dynasties and the Northern Song dynasty have in common?

    a. These dynasties expanded the literate classes.

    b. These dynasties strengthened civil service positions.

    c. These dynasties provided patronage for artists.

3. How did Xia Gui's style differ from the style of earlier Song dynasty landscape painters?

    a. His style was less realistic.

    b. His style was more realistic.

    c. His style had more literal expression.

B Answer the following questions in complete sentences.

1. What were some of the factors involved in the increased support for landscape painters during the Five Dynasties and Northern Song dynasty?

2. How did the developments during the Song dynasty influence art?

3. After 1135, Song rulers became very concerned with internal affairs. How did this focus influence landscape artists?

C On a separate piece of paper, create a chart, flow chart, diagram, or outline to illustrate the information in the reading. Provide a title for your chart, flow chart, diagram, or outline.

Writing about Figures

Examine the figure below. Write a paragraph in which you describe and analyze the painting and the English translation of the poem in the painting. A vocabulary list has been provided. Choose words you need from the list.

aesthetic	composition	landscape	patronage
calligraphy	Confucianism	media	realism
canon	*dao*	monochrome	reverence
commission	depict	nurture	Way of Nature

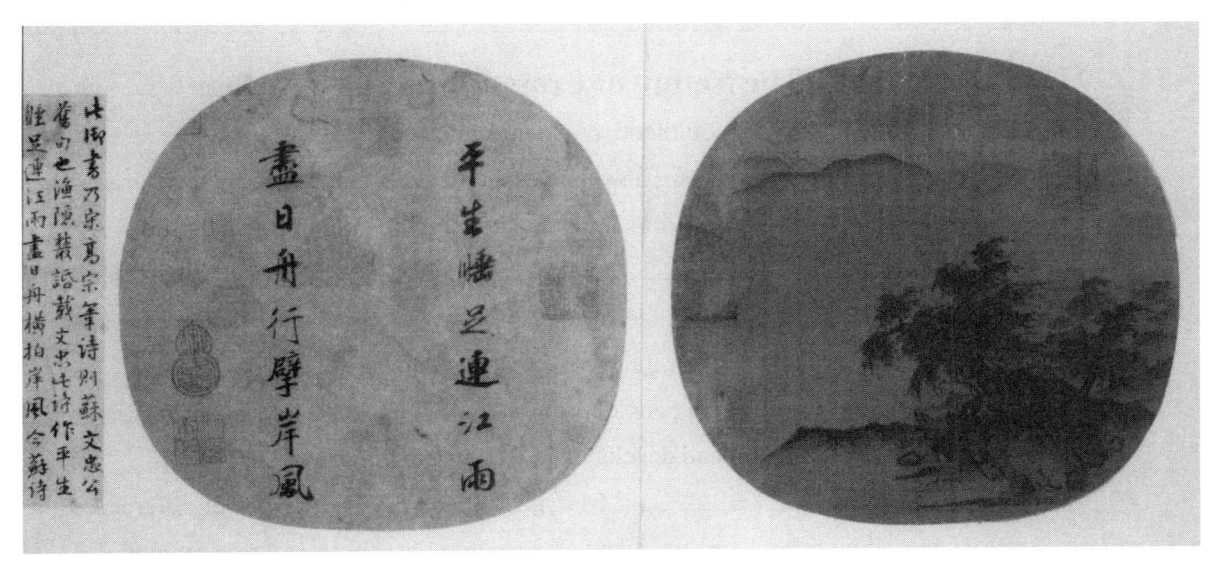

Sailboat in the Rain *by Xia Gui (ca. 1180)*

While sailing through endless rain,
I enjoyed a good sleep.
While boating all day long,
We cut through the wind from the shore.

Name: _____ Date: _____

CHAPTER NINE TEST

Vocabulary

Complete the passage below with words from the following list. Use each word only once. You will not use all the words.

comparative	interactions	psychological universals	traces
culture	manifested	symbolized	traditions
fluctuate	observation	theoretically	various

The Nature of Cross-Cultural Psychology

Before reaching adulthood, most of us do not choose a place to live or a language to speak. People learn how to take action, feel, and understand events around them according to the wishes of their parents, societal requirements, and the (1) _____ of their ancestors. The way people learn to relate to the world through feelings and ideas affects what these individuals do. Their actions, in turn, have a bearing on their thoughts, needs, and emotions.

Conditions in which people live vary from place to place. Human actions and mental sets—formed and developed in various environments—may also (2) _____ from group to group. These kinds of differences—and of course, similarities—are studied by cross-cultural psychology. Cross-cultural psychology is the critical and (3) _____ study of cultural effects on human psychology. Any study in cross-cultural psychology draws its conclusions from at least two samples that represent at least two cultural groups.

Cross-cultural psychology studies cross-cultural (4) _____. For instance, during several centuries, southern and central Spain was under Arab control. How did Islam and Arab culture in general influence the (5) _____ and subsequent behavior, tradition, and values of predominantly Christian Spaniards? Can we find any (6) _____ of Arab influence in individual behavior in Spain and Hispanic cultures today?

Cross-cultural psychology cares not only about differences between cultural groups. It also establishes (7) _____, that is, phenomena common for people in several, many, or perhaps all cultures, such as the structure of human personality—relatively enduring patterns of thinking, feeling, and acting. For example, it was found that the same composition of personality is common in people in (8) _____ countries (such as Germany, Portugal, Israel, China, Korea, and Japan).

Cross-cultural psychological examination is not just a single (9) _____ made by a researcher, psychotherapist, or social worker. Listening to an anecdote or witnessing a vivid event cannot substitute for systematic comparisons of behavior and experience measured under different cultural conditions.

There are perhaps hundreds of definitions of culture. Some of them are elegant and brief, while other definitions are more specific and state that culture is a wide range of settings in which human behavior occurs. Culture is (10) _____ through particular behaviors and values—typically transmitted from generation to generation—and held by individuals of a society.

Reading Comprehension

Read the passage below. As you read, highlight the important ideas and vocabulary used to express those ideas. Annotate the text. Then do the test exercises that follow.

Cross-Cultural Approaches to Studying Human Behavior

Cross-cultural psychologists use a variety of models in their approach to studying human behavior. Some cross-cultural psychologists focus on a particular factor that influences human behavior, while others use a more integrative model which incorporates several approaches.

Sociobiology is a theoretical model that explores the ways in which biological factors affect human behavior and thus lay a natural foundation for human culture. This theoretical paradigm claims that general biological laws of behavior are perfectly suited as a fundamental explanation of human behavior. Culture is just a form of existence that provides for fundamental human needs and subsequent goals. According to this approach, the prime goal of human beings is survival. To endure, humans need food and resources. People look for mates, conceive, give birth, and then protect their offspring until children mature. Humans of all cultures, like animals, try to avoid unnecessary pain and eliminate anything that threatens their well-being.

This is a general view of human behavior that focuses on broad social structures that influence society as a whole, and subsequently its individuals. On the whole, these theories imply that society exists objectively, apart from our individual experience. There are particular social forces that shape the behavior of large social groups, and human beings develop and adjust their individual responses in accordance to the demands and pressures of larger social groups and institutions.

In societies with simple technologies, strong tradition becomes a powerful moral regulator demanding conformity from the society's members. Sharing the same collective conscience, members of such societies penalize those who are different. Everyone is expected to act and think in the same way. This coercive "solidarity" provides people with a powerful sense of belonging. In modern, wealthy societies, on the other hand, discarded traditions break psychological ties among the individuals—like pieces in a broken vase. A huge variety of specializations in the society should make people bond back together. They are interested in relying on one another, but this confidence is based on specialization and diversity and not on tradition or survival needs.

The views of another prominent social scientist, Max Weber, are represented in the symbolic-interactionist approach to understanding society and the individual within it. According to Weber (1922), preindustrial societies develop traditions. Passing traditions on from generation to generation, these societies evaluate particular actions of individuals as either appropriate or inappropriate. Capitalist societies, on the contrary, endorse rationality. Rationality is a deliberate assessment of the most efficient ways of accomplishing a particular goal. Reason defeats emotions, calculation replaces intuition, and scientific analysis eliminates speculation.

According to this crossdisciplinary comprehensive approach, the individual cannot be separated from his or her environmental context. People constantly exchange messages with the environment, thus transforming it and themselves. In other words, these interactions are reciprocal. The individual is seen not as a passive and static entity influenced by the environment, but as a dynamic human being who interacts with and changes the environment. For example, parents educate their children and at the same time their children educate them.

According to the *ecocultural approach*, human environment is a part of a larger cultural system. Both the environment and the individual are seen as open and interchanging systems. Each individual's development takes place within a particular "developmental niche" that can be viewed as a combination of various settings. First there are physical and social settings in which the individual lives: the people, the available products, and services. Second, there are collections of customary practices that convey messages to and from the individual. Finally, there are caretakers' beliefs and expectations about children and their rearing. These three types of settings mediate the individual's development within the larger culture.

To combine and critically apply these—and possibly other approaches to cross-cultural psychology—let us introduce two general concepts: **activity** and **availability of resources**. For the cross-cultural psychologist, human behavior is not only a "result" or "product" of cultural influences. People are also free, active, and rational individuals who are capable of exercising their own will. **Activity** is a process of the individual's goal-directed interaction with the environment. Human motivation, emotion, thought, and reactions cannot be separated from human activity, which is (1) determined by individual, socioeconomic, environmental, political, and cultural conditions and also (2) changes in these conditions. In fact, human psychology develops within human activity and manifests through it. Imagine, for example, a child who grows up in a zone of an ethnic conflict and for whom survival becomes a primary activity. He or she develops emotions, motivation, and cognitive processes quite different from those children who grew up in safe conditions. At the same time, because this child can also engage in activities similar for children in most environments—like playing, learning arithmetic, thinking about the future, helping parents, to name a few—the child will be likely to share many common psychological characteristics with his or her counterparts around the world. Cultures may be similar and different in terms of the most common activities of their members.

Presence of and access to resources essential for the individual's well-being largely determine type, scope, and direction of human activities. There are societies with plenty of resources available and there are regions in which resources are extremely scarce. Geographic location, climate, natural disasters, or absence of such may determine how much resources are available to individuals.

A Circle the correct answers.

1. How do sociobiologists describe culture?

    a. The purpose of culture is to help people survive.

    b. The purpose of culture is to develop a society.

    c. The purpose of culture is to help people find mates.

2. What did Max Weber believe about people in capitalist societies?

    a. They do not evaluate each other's actions.

    b. They have eliminated all their traditions.

    c. They try to use reason in making decisions.

3. According to the author, what happens to a child who grows up in an area of ethnic conflict?

    a. The child develops psychological problems relating to survival.

    b. The child may still be similar to other children in different situations.

    c. The child develops motivations that are not helpful when the situation improves.

B Answer the following questions in complete sentences.

1. What aspects of human behavior are not explained by the sociobiological approach to studying human behavior?

2. The author states that in capitalist societies, people make decisions based on reason, calculation, and scientific analysis. Do you agree or disagree with the author? Explain your reasons for your answer.

3. What are some ways that availability of resources might determine human activity?

C On a separate piece of paper, create a chart, flow chart, diagram, or outline to illustrate the information in the reading. Provide a title for your chart, flow chart, diagram, or outline.

Writing about Figures

Examine the figure below. Write a paragraph in which you describe the activities of the people in the photograph in light of the concepts you have learned in this chapter. A vocabulary list has been provided. Choose words you need from the list.

access to resources	explicit characteristics	overt
availability	implicit characteristics	rationality
culture	interact	Social Darwinism
ecological context	manifest	tradition

Women from a village in Senegal, Africa, drawing water from a well

Name: _____ Date: _____

CHAPTER TEN TEST

Vocabulary

Complete the passage below with words from the following list. Use each word only once. You will not use all the words.

biological	individual	scarce	survive
collective	natural selection	sociobiologists	theories
correlations	promote	sociological	universal

Motivation and Behavior

Motivation is a condition—usually an internal one—that initiates, activates, or maintains the individual's goal-directed behavior. The nature of human motivation is a subject of discussions and continuous attempts to find a (1) _____ theory that would explain it. (2) _____, for example, generally believe that biological factors best explain social behavior. Some (3) _____ theories claim the nature of human motivation is social or economic. Classical psychologists have also contributed to the theory of motivation by determining major psychological mechanisms that underlie basic human needs. Let us briefly examine several well-established (4) _____ of motivation. A critical examination of these approaches provides cross-cultural psychologists with valuable ideas that can be used to analyze specific kinds of human motivation.

The origin of human motivation is biological, according to sociobiology. Human beings make rational decisions, develop arts and sciences, and build up modern technologies. Still, despite obvious cultural and economic achievements, people remain a part of the larger biological universe. Above all, people need to survive. The (5) _____ principle, first described by Charles Darwin in the nineteenth century, becomes a key interpreter of human behavior in sociobiology. Due to genetic variations, some organisms are more likely to survive than others. Those who (6) _____ pass on their "advantageous" genes to their offspring. Over many generations, genetic patterns that (7) _____ survival become dominant. For instance, hunters become successful seekers and killers of animals and gatherers become excellent finders of berries, roots, and fruit. Herbert Spencer asserted that the struggle for survival within the human species motivates people to compete for (8) _____ resources. Individuals who are skillful competitors, who are fit for the struggle, will succeed and prosper. The unfit, or those who lack the motivation to compete, will fail.

Survival needs can be individual and collective. Baldwin, for example, suggested that the principle of (9) _____ survival is part of the psychology of African people. Continued existence of the group—and not necessarily (10) _____ survival—is closely linked to the collective responsibility and interdependence of Africans. The sociobiological approach to human motivation generally fails to explain the diversity of human needs and overlooks the influence of social, cultural, and religious factors.

Reading Comprehension

Read the passage below. As you read, highlight the important ideas and vocabulary used to express those ideas. Annotate the text. Then do the test exercises that follow.

Universal Mechanisms of Human Motivation

Cognitive theories maintain that people are aware of their thought patterns and therefore can control their motivation and behavior. People learn what they want and how to achieve rewards, mastery, and affiliation. There are two types of motivation: intrinsic and extrinsic. **Intrinsic motivation** engages people in various activities for no apparent reward except the pleasure and satisfaction of the activity itself. Edward Deci (1972) suggested that people engage in such behaviors for two reasons: to obtain cognitive stimulation and to gain a sense of accomplishment, competency, and mastery over the environment. In contrast, **extrinsic motivation** comes from the external environment. Examples of extrinsic rewards include praise, a high grade, or money given for a particular behavior. Such rewards can strengthen existing behaviors, provide people with information about their performance, and increase feelings of self-worth. In childhood, people begin to learn about both intrinsic and extrinsic rewards. For example, in one study it was found that educated American children displayed a stronger capacity for delaying their expectations for an immediate reward than less educated children, who showed the opposite trend (Doob, 1971). Differences in gender socialization may cause different motivational outcomes. A study of American, Polish, and German children (Boehnke et al., 1989) showed that in all three samples girls preferred intrinsic motives more frequently than boys. Perhaps achievement-oriented motivation was part of the socialization of the boys in the studied nations. Emphasizing the importance of learning and rational choice, cognitive theories can be useful in cross-cultural research. Let us now examine achievement motivation.

People constantly strive for achievement and excellence. Take a look at masterpieces of human creativity such as the pyramids in Egypt and the Eiffel tower in Paris. Turn to a sports channel on television and see how athletes of different national, religious, and ethnic backgrounds compete for excellence. Read the poetry of Nizami, the great son of Persia, and any novel written by literary genius Gabriel García Márquez of Colombia. People try to achieve what others could not. **Need for achievement** is a social need that directs people to constantly strive for excellence and success, influence, and accomplishment. Activities not oriented toward these goals are not motivating and are usually performed without commitment. Are we born with such motivation to achieve?

One of the early leaders in early studies of achievement motivation, David McClelland (1958), gave a categorical "no" to this question. He demonstrated that achievement motivation is learned during childhood. It might be acquired from parents who stress excellence and display affection and emotional rewards to their children for high levels of achievement. During the individual's life, a wide range of social and psychological factors could further influence achievement motivation. If there is no such example set for the child, he or she will not develop the need for achievement.

Particular social norms may be linked to this motivation. In a classic research study on motivation, McClelland (1987) analyzed children's stories in 22 cultures with respect to the degree to which the stories showed themes of achievement motivation. He then related these levels of motivation to measures of economic development in the studied countries. Achievement motivation scores were highly correlated with economic growth of the children's countries. In other words, the greater the emphasis placed on achievement in the stories told to children in various nations, the more rapid the economic development in these nations as the children grew up.

In a cross-national project that involved more than 12,000 participants, Furnham et al. (1994) also showed a strong relationship between individual achievement motivation and economic growth. In particular, economic growth correlated with attitudes toward competitiveness. The stronger these attitudes, the higher the achievement motivation. The higher the achievement motivation, the greater the rate of economic growth. It shouldn't take much imagination to realize that any two individuals may develop two different types of achievement motivation: low and high. One strives for excellence and success, the other is happy doing what is required and does not need recognition from others. What definitely is intriguing is the idea of cultural differences in motivation. Do the results of the studies mentioned previously suggest that there are high- and low-achievement-oriented nations and cultures?

This question brings the debate about cultural differences in achievement motivation to a new level. They key to the answer is that achievement or success can be understood in several ways. So-called **individualist-success motivation**—the type of motivation measured in most studies cited so far—affects one's attitudes and actions and is directed to the attainment of personal goals. On the contrary, **collectivist-success motivation** directs a person to connect with other people; the individual's contribution is seen as beneficial to the members of a particular group or society in general (Parsons & Goff, 1978).

Each society chooses standards for excellence and always determines what type of goals—individual or collective—a person is expected to achieve. The individualist type prevails among people in Western cultures, such as the United States, France, and Germany. The collectivist type is more common in Eastern cultures, such as India, Korea, and Japan (Maehr & Nicholls, 1983). In Japan, for example, striving for success is motivated more often by a concern for the reaction of others than by the pursuit of personal satisfaction (Gallimore, 1974). Within Chinese culture, collective achievement orientation is regarded as most valuable (Yand, 1986). In Korea, Thailand, and China, there is a special kind of work ethic, according to which future-oriented and harmonious interpersonal networks are essential for business success (Cho & Kim, 1993). It was also found that Australian Aboriginal students placed greater emphasis on collectivist intentions, compared with non-Aboriginal students (Fogarty & White, 1994). Cross-cultural psychologists continue to study a range of cultures, and to learn more about the nature of human motivation.

A Circle the correct answers.

1. What conclusion can cross-cultural psychologists draw about social norms?

    a. They are always the same among different cultures.

    b. They are always different among different cultures.

    c. They are an influencing factor in children's development.

2. In the 22 cultures studies, what was one of the purposes of children's stories?

    a. to help children learn about the world

    b. to provide examples of appropriate behavior

    c. to make children do what their parents wish

3. What kind of behavior does achievement motivation appear to be?

    a. mostly learned

    b. mostly instinctive

    c. partly instinctive and partly learned

B Answer the following questions in complete sentences.

1. Why might level of education influence a child's ability to delay expectations for an immediate reward?

   _____
   _____
   _____

2. Do all people have a need for achievement? Explain your reasons for your answer.

   _____
   _____
   _____

3. Can individualist-success motivation and collectivist-success motivation both be found in the same culture? Explain your reasons for your answer.

   _____
   _____
   _____

C On a separate piece of paper, create a chart, flow chart, diagram, or outline to illustrate the information in the reading. Provide a title for your chart, flow chart, diagram, or outline.

Writing about Figures

Examine the figures below. Write a paragraph in which you discuss possible motivation for the behavior of the people in the two photographs. A vocabulary list has been provided. Choose words you need from the list.

diversity	imitate	promote
fulfillment	initiate	self-actualization
hierarchy of needs	motivation	stimuli
humanistic theories	natural selection	survival

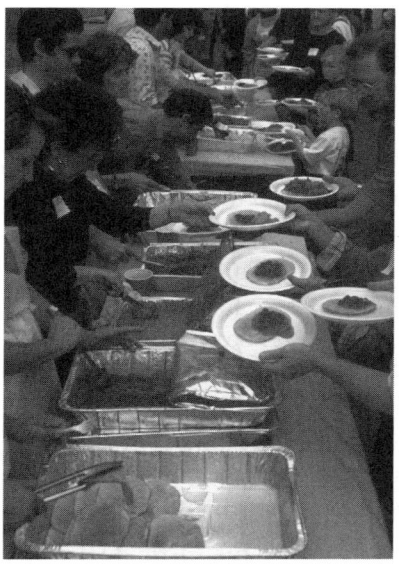

Volunteers serving Christmas dinner to the homeless, Los Angeles, California

A group of sixteen blind hikers from Japan, South Korea, and Taiwan celebrate after reaching the peak of Jade Mountain in Taiwan (1999)

Answer Key to the Tests

CHAPTER ONE TEST

Vocabulary

1. adaptive   2. species   3. predators   4. survive   5. motivations
6. Behavior   7. value   8. exploiting   9. dominance   10. respond

Reading Comprehension

A. 1. c   2. b   3. a

B. 1. The squirrel's behavior is learned. People who came to the park and sat on benches probably threw food to the squirrel as it happened to pass by. Over time and with experience, the squirrel began to associate, or connect, people eating on park benches with receiving food. This is an example of associative learning.

2. This activity is an example of instinctive behavior. The adult bird is programmed to respond to the stimulus of hearing its babies make sounds and opening their mouths with a feeding response. This activity is done correctly the first time, without prior experience.

3. This activity is an example of learned behavior. The elephants could not know about the second watering hole without prior experience. They probably used that watering hole in the past and remembered its location.

4. This activity is an example of instinctive behavior. For the turtle, feeling a touch on its head is a stimulus. The turtle's reaction is to pull its head into its shell to protect itself. This action is performed correctly every time.

C. Students' choices of format may vary but should be organized in a logical manner, include the key ideas in the reading, and make use of appropriate vocabulary, as in the example below.

A Comparison of Instinctive and Learned Behavior		
Type of Behavior	**Description**	**Advantages / Disadvantages**
instinctive	<ul><li>inborn, preprogrammed, automatic, inflexible, genetically determined</li><li>performed correctly the first time without previous experience when proper stimulus is given</li><li>most common in animals with short life cycles, simple nervous systems, little contact with parents</li><li>most animals have high proportion of instinctive behavior</li></ul>	<ul><li>advantage: can ensure survival if it is involved in basic, essential activities</li><li>disadvantage: behavior cannot be modified when a new situation arises</li></ul>
learned	<ul><li>requires experience</li><li>produces behaviors that can be changed</li><li>significant in long-lived animals that care for their young</li><li>young imitate parents and develop appropriate behaviors</li><li>requires a large brain to store new information</li><li>many birds and mammals demonstrate a great deal of learned behavior</li></ul>	<ul><li>advantage: animals that live many years benefit from the ability to recognize previously encountered situations and modify their behavior when needed</li><li>advantage: behavior is adaptable</li></ul>

Writing about Figures

Students' writing may vary but should accurately reflect the information in the chapter and in the photographs, make use of appropriate vocabulary, and be grammatically correct.

CHAPTER TWO TEST

Vocabulary

1. imitate   2. isolated   3. species   4. refinements   5. instinct
6. innate   7. invertebrates   8. whereas   9. vertebrates   10. components

Reading Comprehension

A. 1. association   2. insight   3. imprinting

B. 1. Students' answers will vary but should demonstrate a clear understanding of associative learning.

2. Students' answers may vary. Possible answers are: Imprinting is a very limited type of learning for such a complex organism as a human being. There are few instances when imprinting would be an advantage to us. Imprinting involves a type of learning that cannot be unlearned, and is therefore inflexible. For humans who are continuously encountering new situations, imprinting could become a big disadvantage.

3. Students' answers may vary. Possible answers are that an individual member of a species might not be able to gain any territory. As a result, it may not be healthy because it does not get sufficient food, it may die, or it may survive but not reproduce. However, the stronger members of the species will have sufficient food, remain healthy, and reproduce. Since the stronger members reproduce, the species as a whole benefits.

C. Students' choices of format may vary but should be organized in a logical manner, include the key ideas in the reading, and make use of appropriate vocabulary, as in the example below.

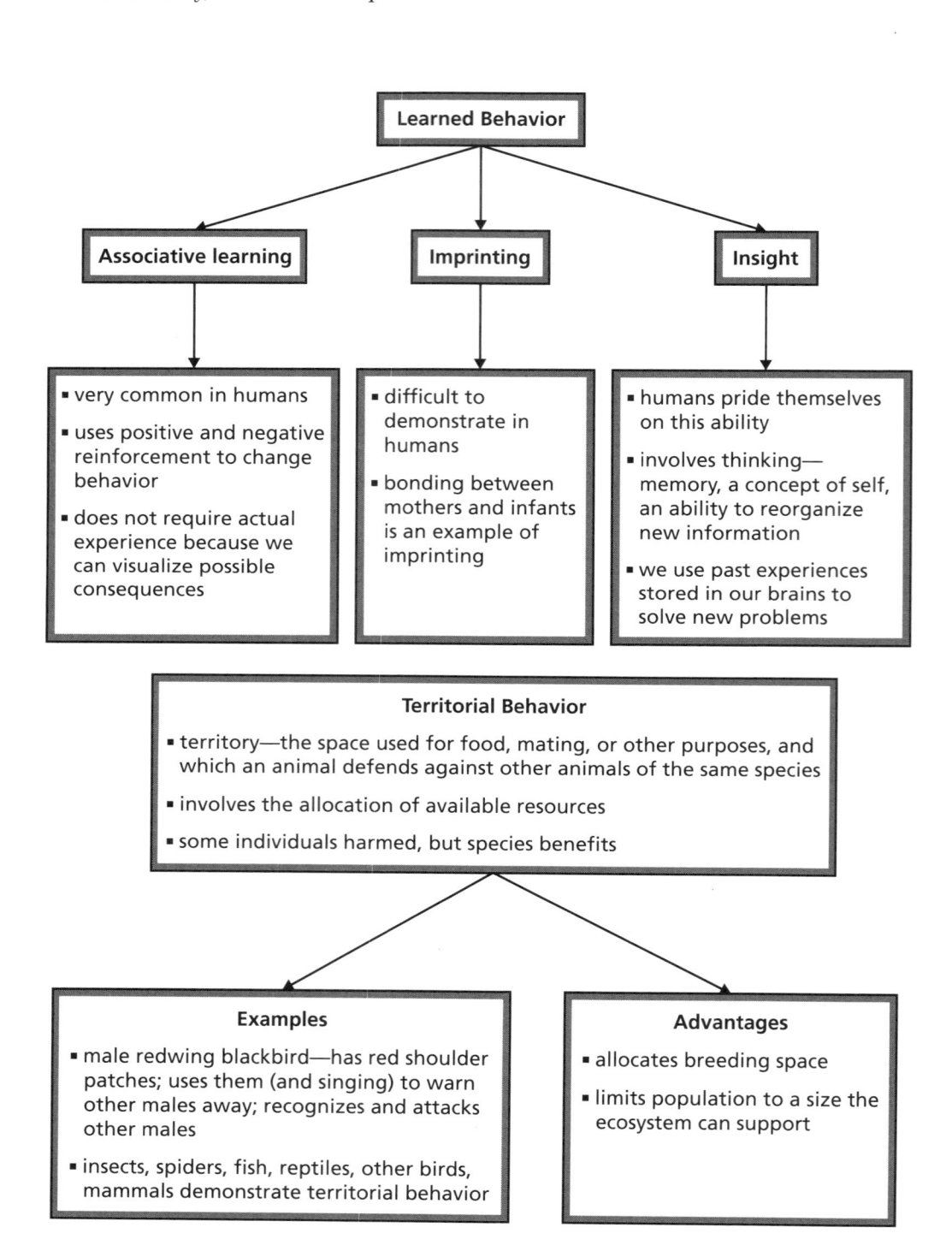

Learned Behavior

- **Associative learning**
  - very common in humans
  - uses positive and negative reinforcement to change behavior
  - does not require actual experience because we can visualize possible consequences

- **Imprinting**
  - difficult to demonstrate in humans
  - bonding between mothers and infants is an example of imprinting

- **Insight**
  - humans pride themselves on this ability
  - involves thinking—memory, a concept of self, an ability to reorganize new information
  - we use past experiences stored in our brains to solve new problems

Territorial Behavior
- territory—the space used for food, mating, or other purposes, and which an animal defends against other animals of the same species
- involves the allocation of available resources
- some individuals harmed, but species benefits

Examples
- male redwing blackbird—has red shoulder patches; uses them (and singing) to warn other males away; recognizes and attacks other males
- insects, spiders, fish, reptiles, other birds, mammals demonstrate territorial behavior

Advantages
- allocates breeding space
- limits population to a size the ecosystem can support

Writing about Figures

Students' writing may vary but should accurately reflect the information in the chapter and in the photographs, make use of appropriate vocabulary, and be grammatically correct.

CHAPTER THREE TEST

Vocabulary

1. expressed   2. stimuli   3. feature   4. taboo   5. cultural
6. variable   7. concept   8. passive   9. active   10. transmitted

Reading Comprehension

A. 1. a   2. c   3. b   4. c

B. 1. A cultural group codifies its world view by making assumptions about the way things are, and then talking about them, sharing them, and passing them on to others.

2. The Netsilik take such care with the bodies of the animals they kill because they do not want the dead animals' souls to become evil, or to offend living animals.

3. The invention of farming enabled these people to gain direct control over their food source, and so made them less dependent on the supernatural. Because of this, they changed their view of the world and their place in it.

4. People tend to move from polytheistic beliefs to monotheistic beliefs when they begin to have a sense of control over the world around them.

(The answers continue on the next page.)

C. Students' choices of format may vary but should be organized in a logical manner, include the key ideas in the reading, and make use of appropriate vocabulary, as in the example below.

How the World View of Two Cultures Is Reflected in Their Religious Beliefs		
Culture	**Environment and Food Sources**	**Beliefs**
Netsilik (Eskimo)	<ul><li>live in the Arctic</li><li>very harsh environment</li><li>are well adapted to their environment</li><li>have little control over nature</li><li>hunt seal and caribou</li></ul>	<ul><li>see themselves as one with the land and its life</li><li>consider animals as part of their community</li><li>believe that the spirit world controls the natural world</li><li>believe that animals have spirits/souls</li><li>are polytheistic</li><li>souls are unreliable and can become evil</li><li>have rituals to treat animals they kill</li><li>pour water in dead seal's mouth because soul is thirsty</li><li>do not work on killed caribou where other caribou can see them</li></ul>
Southwest Asians 10,000 years ago	<ul><li>had some control over nature</li><li>invented farming</li></ul>	<ul><li>farming made them feel in control over their food sources</li><li>were monotheistic</li><li>had some sense of personal control when dealing with the supernatural</li><li>felt they could know and understand the world around them, and use the knowledge to control their world</li></ul>

Writing about Figures

Students' writing may vary but should accurately reflect the information in the chapter and in the photographs, make use of appropriate vocabulary, and be grammatically correct.

CHAPTER FOUR TEST

Vocabulary

1. world view   2. trait   3. expression   4. variation   5. Polytheism
6. interact   7. Monotheistic   8. intervenes   9. phenomena   10. supernatural

Reading Comprehension

A. 1. d   2. c   3. a   4. e   5. b

B. 1. Students' answers may vary but should make sense and should demonstrate understanding of the principles of discovery and invention.

2. Students' answers may vary. Possible answers are: Cultures might change so rapidly that the change causes a breakdown in the social structure of the group; in an egalitarian society, some people in the society might become disadvantaged if they cannot benefit from the artifacts that are borrowed from the other culture; valued traditions in the society might be endangered when a new idea or concept is introduced into the culture.

3. Students' answers may vary. A possible answer is: Yes, the automobile can be considered a revolution. It led to the development of complex road and highway systems, and to the increased mobility of people; people were able to work and travel much farther than they ever had before; travel and tourism increased dramatically; the car became a symbol of wealth, luxury, and freedom.

(The answers continue on the next page.)

C. Students' choices of format may vary but should be organized in a logical manner, include the key ideas in the reading, and make use of appropriate vocabulary, as in the example below.

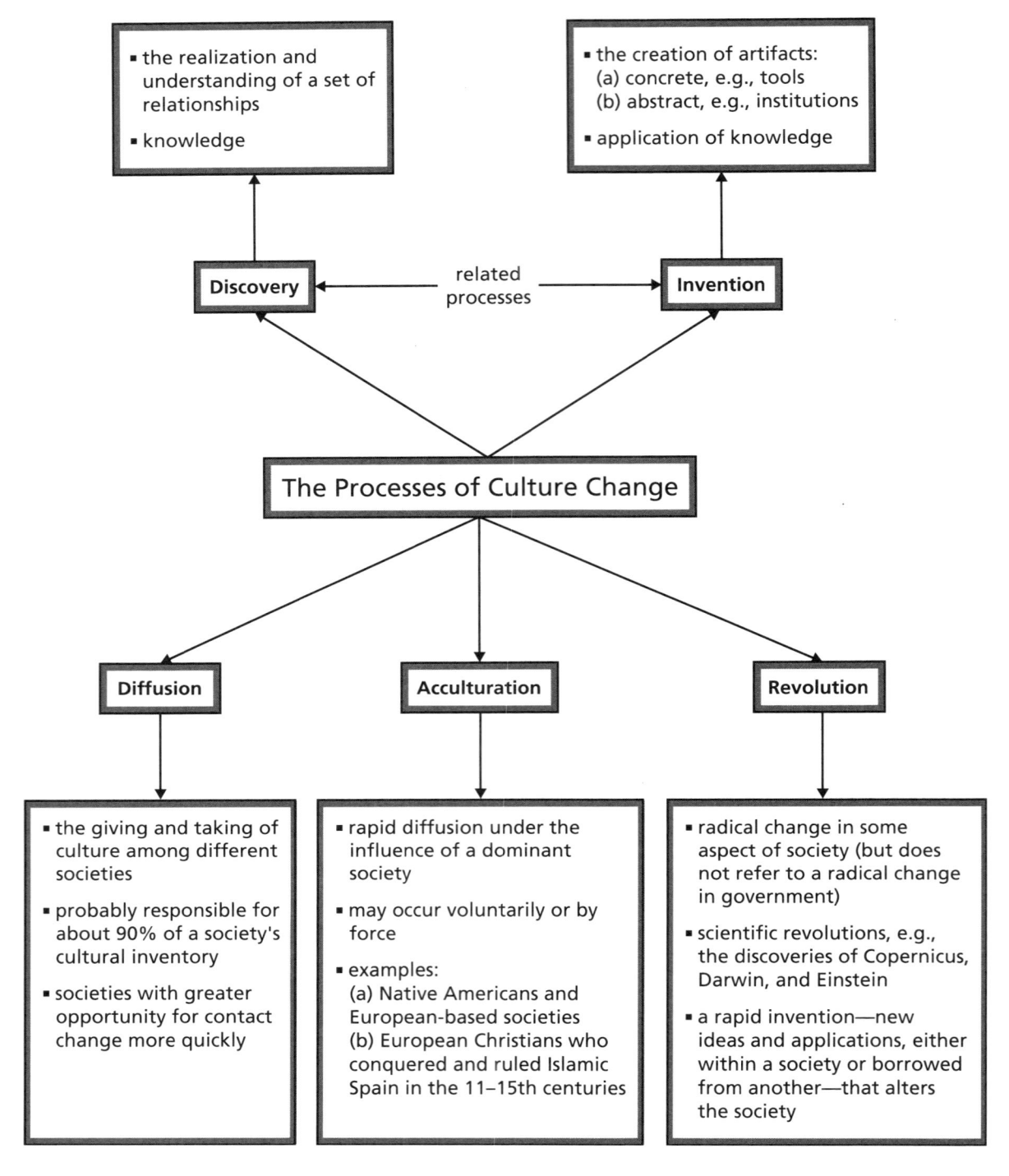

```
┌─────────────────────────────┐           ┌─────────────────────────────┐
│ • the realization and       │           │ • the creation of artifacts:│
│   understanding of a set of │           │   (a) concrete, e.g., tools │
│   relationships             │           │   (b) abstract, e.g.,       │
│ • knowledge                 │           │       institutions          │
│                             │           │ • application of knowledge  │
└──────────────┬──────────────┘           └──────────────┬──────────────┘
               ▲                                         ▲
               │                                         │
          ┌─────────┐      related         ┌──────────┐
          │Discovery│◄─── processes ────►  │Invention │
          └─────────┘                      └──────────┘
                ▲                                  ▲
                 \                                /
                  \                              /
                   \     ┌──────────────────┐  /
                    └───►│ The Processes of │◄─┘
                         │  Culture Change  │
                         └────────┬─────────┘
             ┌────────────────────┼────────────────────┐
             ▼                    ▼                    ▼
        ┌─────────┐         ┌────────────┐        ┌──────────┐
        │Diffusion│         │Acculturation│       │Revolution│
        └────┬────┘         └──────┬─────┘        └────┬─────┘
             ▼                     ▼                   ▼
```

Diffusion	Acculturation	Revolution
• the giving and taking of culture among different societies • probably responsible for about 90% of a society's cultural inventory • societies with greater opportunity for contact change more quickly	• rapid diffusion under the influence of a dominant society • may occur voluntarily or by force • examples: (a) Native Americans and European-based societies (b) European Christians who conquered and ruled Islamic Spain in the 11–15th centuries	• radical change in some aspect of society (but does not refer to a radical change in government) • scientific revolutions, e.g., the discoveries of Copernicus, Darwin, and Einstein • a rapid invention—new ideas and applications, either within a society or borrowed from another—that alters the society

Writing about Figures

Students' writing may vary but should accurately reflect the information in the chapter and in the illustrations, make use of appropriate vocabulary, and be grammatically correct.

CHAPTER FIVE TEST

Vocabulary

1. Scholarship   2. doctrine   3. astonishing   4. perplexing   5. experimentation
6. revolved   7. Aristotle   8. contradictions   9. observation   10. Galileo

Reading Comprehension

A.   1. c   2. a   3. b

B.   1. In scientific experimentation, it is essential to repeat the same experiment many times to be sure you are getting the same results, so you can generate a theory, or a hypothesis, about what you are observing.

2. Galileo based his theorizing on observations and experimentation, whereas Aristotle based his theories on common sense and on views of the spiritual and moral worlds.

3. Copernicus's biggest contribution to the Scientific Revolution was his proposal that the sun and not the Earth is at the center of the universe because this idea stimulated other astronomers to make new calculations and thus to discover new information.

C.   Students' choices of format may vary but should be organized in a logical manner, include the key ideas in the reading, and make use of appropriate vocabulary, as in the example below.

THE NEW SEVENTEENTH-CENTURY SCIENCE AND ARISTOTLE'S TEACHINGS		
The New Science	**Aristotle**	**Copernicus**
▪ was materialistic—the universe is composed of matter in motion ▪ stars, planets, and earth are made of the same matter ▪ was mathematical—to understand the universe, calculation has to replace common sense ▪ used experimentation to understand the universe	▪ his understanding of the physical world coincided with the spiritual and moral world ▪ his world view could be incorporated into Christianity ▪ the heavens are perfect and unchanging, better than earth ▪ problem: if planets revolve in circles, why do they appear closer or farther, brighter or darker at different times?	▪ 1490s—hypothesized that sun is at the center of the universe ▪ sun-centered hypothesis predicted position of planets slightly better ▪ his sun-centered theory stimulated others to make new calculations

Writing about Figures

Students' writing may vary but should accurately reflect the information in the chapter and in the illustration, make use of appropriate vocabulary, and be grammatically correct.

CHAPTER SIX TEST

Vocabulary

1. Scientific Revolution 2. telescope 3. credence 4. instrument 5. enumerate
6. terrestrial 7. celestial 8. hemisphere 9. observation 10. prominences

Reading Comprehension

A. 1. c 2. b 3. a

B. 1. Aristotle believed that all heavenly objects revolve around the Earth. Galileo discovered that Jupiter had four moons that revolved around Jupiter. Therefore, Aristotle's belief was disproved.

2. Galileo believed that his discoveries did not go against what was written in the Bible. He believed that it was sometimes difficult to interpret what was written in the Bible, and that nature was a way that God revealed himself.

3. Newton's concept of universal gravitation was so important to science because it enabled scientists to create scientific laws that apply to everything in the universe. They did not need to create different sets of laws of motion for objects on Earth and for objects in the heavens.

C. Students' choices of format may vary but should be organized in a logical manner, include the key ideas in the reading, and make use of appropriate vocabulary, as in the example below.

Scientists Who Studied the Universe and Disproved the Old Cosmology

I. Tycho Brahe (1546–1601)—Danish
   A. His discovery of a nova disproved the idea of an unchanging universe.
   B. He believed that all the planets except for the Earth revolved around the sun, and they all revolved around the Earth.

II. Johannes Kepler (1571–1630)—(his nationality is not stated in the text)
   A. He created laws of planetary motion.
   B. He discovered the elliptical orbits of the planets. This disproved the circular orbit theory.
   C. He showed a mathematical relationship between the speed of a planet's revolution and its distance from the sun.
   D. His findings supported heliocentrism.
   E. His findings supported the view that the entire universe is made of matter that is subject to physical laws.

III. Galileo Galilei (1564–1642)—Italian
   A. In 1610, he discovered four moons of Jupiter. This discovery disproved the belief that everything in the universe revolved around the sun.
   B. Using a telescope, he showed that the surface of the moon is imperfect, and he discovered spots on the sun. These discoveries proved that the universe is imperfect.
   C. In 1616, the Church warned him not to talk about his views.
   D. In 1633, he was tried by the Inquisition, and lived the rest of his life under house arrest.
   E. Galileo never intended to reject the Bible.

IV. Sir Isaac Newton (1642–1727)—English
  A. He solved the problem, "What is motion?"
  B. He formulated the concept of force.
  C. He developed laws of motion.
     1. Objects at rest or in uniform linear motion remain that way unless acted on by an external force.
     2. Changes in motion are proportional to force.
     3. For every action there is an equal and opposite reaction.
  D. He developed the concept of a universal gravitation that governed the movement of all objects, from an apple to a planet.

Writing about Figures

Students' writing may vary but should accurately reflect the information in the chapter and in the photograph, make use of appropriate vocabulary, and be grammatically correct.

CHAPTER SEVEN TEST

Vocabulary

1. artists   2. incorporating   3. perspective   4. representations   5. antiquity

6. Renaissance   7. Middle Ages   8. models   9. inspiration   10. impetus

Reading Comprehension

A. 1. b   2. d   3. a   4. e   5. c

B. 1. People demonstrated the dignity of the individual and the new self-consciousness by changing their views about artists. Artists were considered trained intellectuals. They were made famous, signed their work, and even wrote autobiographies.

2. The new concept of humanism changed artists' subjects by making the individual important so that people wanted paintings of themselves and their families, and other decorations, for their homes.

3. The main difference between Italian art and Flemish art was that classical Roman and Greek art influenced Italian art, but not Flemish art, which focused on everyday subjects.

(The answers continue on the next page.)

C. Students' choices of format may vary but should be organized in a logical manner, include the key ideas in the reading, and make use of appropriate vocabulary, as in the example below.

```
┌─────────────────────────────────────────────────────┐
│  Renaissance Art and the Concept of Humanism        │
└─────────────────────────────────────────────────────┘
```

Humanism
- inspired by ideas in ancient Greek and Roman texts
- included praise for deeds of great figures from Greek and Roman antiquity
- supported idea of pride and fame
- promoted the dignity of the individual

In Italy
- artists became famous;
  - —they signed their work
  - —Lorenzo Ghiberti wrote his autobiography
- there were many secular and religious commissions
  - —rulers, city governments, and individuals all commissioned art
  - —subjects included models from antiquity, portraits, mythological subjects, and secular decorations
- scientific perspective was an innovation
  - —Filippo Brunelleschi solved the problem of perspective
  - —parallel lines that recede into the distance seem to converge at a point on the horizon
  - —examples: *The Trinity with the Virgin Mary, Saint John, and Two Donors* by Masaccio, and *Christ Giving the Keys to Saint Peter* by Perugino

In Flanders
- artists became famous, too
- the Flemish were not interested in ancient Greek and Roman art or subjects
- the *Très Riches Heures du Duc de Berry* by the Limboug brothers characterizes Flemish realism
  - —shows people and scenes in a natural way
  - —offers atmospheric effects
  - —is an example of the study of natural phenomena
  - —was admired and copied by later artists

Writing about Figures

Students' writing may vary but should accurately reflect the information in the chapter and in the painting, make use of appropriate vocabulary, and be grammatically correct.

CHAPTER EIGHT TEST

Vocabulary

1. nurtured   2. patronage   3. calligraphy   4. aesthetic   5. depicted
6. Way of Nature   7. canons   8. composition   9. reverence   10. representing

Reading Comprehension

A. 1. b   2. c   3. a

B. 1. Some of the factors involved in the increased support for landscape painters during these periods were the increase in scholars because books became less expensive and more available, an empire that was unified without war, and the fact that the rulers were more interested in art.

2. Developments during the Song dynasty influenced art through *li*, which governed how a painting was composed. Artists were expected to be faithful to nature and to use conventionalized symbols.

3. After 1135, when Song rulers were more interested in internal affairs, artists focused on painting what was nearby and up close, rather than on larger landscapes.

C. Students' choices of format may vary but should be organized in a logical manner, include the key ideas in the reading, and make use of appropriate vocabulary, as in the example below.

Chinese Landscape Painters in the Tenth–Twelfth Centuries

I. Li Cheng (active from about 940 to 967)

   A. represented the ideal Chinese painter
   B. was educated in humanities; painted for his own delight; was a scholar
   D. preferred autumnal or wintry scenes; monochrome ink; small brush strokes (*cun*)
   E. art aimed for truth to natural appearance; used shifting perspective

II. Five Dynasties (907–960) and North Song Dynasty (960–1126)

   A. *Classical Texts* was printed in 952; books became inexpensive and abundant
   B. many more scholars than before
   C. renaissance of literature; formation of neo-Confucianism
   D. *li* was moral law, an ethical code; included painting faithful to nature
   E. 1135—Song court established new capital in Hangzhou; academy of painting was reestablished; new painting style evolved
   F. Xia Gui and other artists developed a less literal and more suggestive style of painting

Writing about Figures

Students' writing may vary but should accurately reflect the information in the chapter and in the painting, make use of appropriate vocabulary, and be grammatically correct.

CHAPTER NINE TEST

Vocabulary

1. traditions   2. fluctuate   3. comparative   4. interactions   5. culture
6. traces   7. psychological universals   8. various   9. observation   10. manifested

Reading Comprehension

A. 1. a   2. c   3. b

B. Students' answers to these three questions may vary but all answers should make sense and reflect an understanding of the reading. Possible answers for numbers 1 and 3 are:

1. The sociobiological approach does not explain human behaviors that are not directed towards survival. For example, art, telling stories, and playing games are part of many cultures, but they do not help an individual or a group survive.

3. When resources are available, people might engage in more activities that are not directly related to survival, whereas when resources are scarce, people will spend more time trying to find or save limited resources.

C. Students' choices of format may vary but should be organized in a logical manner, include the key ideas in the reading, and make use of appropriate vocabulary, as in the example below.

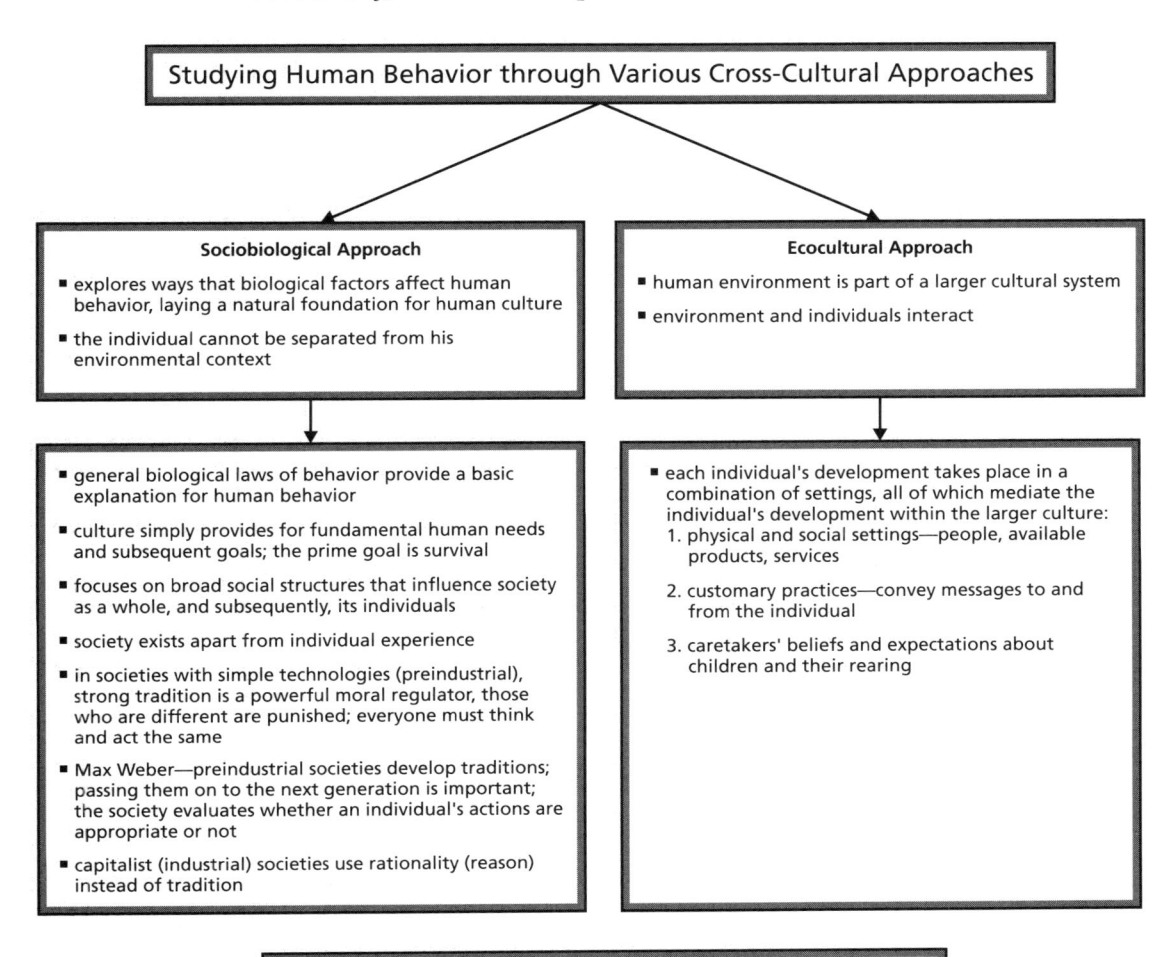

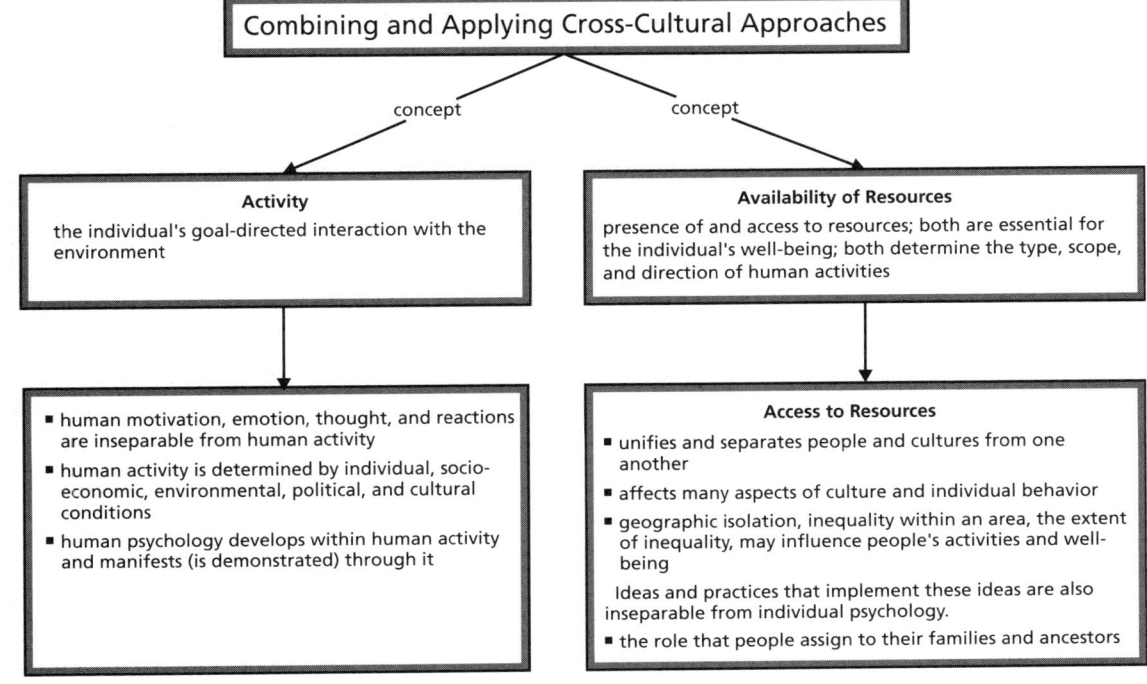

Studying Human Behavior through Various Cross-Cultural Approaches

Sociobiological Approach
- explores ways that biological factors affect human behavior, laying a natural foundation for human culture
- the individual cannot be separated from his environmental context

- general biological laws of behavior provide a basic explanation for human behavior
- culture simply provides for fundamental human needs and subsequent goals; the prime goal is survival
- focuses on broad social structures that influence society as a whole, and subsequently, its individuals
- society exists apart from individual experience
- in societies with simple technologies (preindustrial), strong tradition is a powerful moral regulator, those who are different are punished; everyone must think and act the same
- Max Weber—preindustrial societies develop traditions; passing them on to the next generation is important; the society evaluates whether an individual's actions are appropriate or not
- capitalist (industrial) societies use rationality (reason) instead of tradition

Ecocultural Approach
- human environment is part of a larger cultural system
- environment and individuals interact

- each individual's development takes place in a combination of settings, all of which mediate the individual's development within the larger culture:
  1. physical and social settings—people, available products, services
  2. customary practices—convey messages to and from the individual
  3. caretakers' beliefs and expectations about children and their rearing

Combining and Applying Cross-Cultural Approaches

concept → **Activity**
the individual's goal-directed interaction with the environment

concept → **Availability of Resources**
presence of and access to resources; both are essential for the individual's well-being; both determine the type, scope, and direction of human activities

- human motivation, emotion, thought, and reactions are inseparable from human activity
- human activity is determined by individual, socio-economic, environmental, political, and cultural conditions
- human psychology develops within human activity and manifests (is demonstrated) through it

Access to Resources
- unifies and separates people and cultures from one another
- affects many aspects of culture and individual behavior
- geographic isolation, inequality within an area, the extent of inequality, may influence people's activities and well-being

Ideas and practices that implement these ideas are also inseparable from individual psychology.
- the role that people assign to their families and ancestors

Writing about Figures

Students' writing may vary but should accurately reflect the information in the chapter and in the photograph, make use of appropriate vocabulary, and be grammatically correct.

CHAPTER TEN TEST

Vocabulary

1. universal   2. Sociobiologists   3. sociological   4. theories   5. natural selection
6. survive   7. promote   8. scarce   9. collective   10. individual

Reading Comprehension

A.   1. c   2. b   3. a

B.   Students' answers to these three questions may vary but all three answers should make sense and reflect an understanding of the reading. A possible answer for question 1 is that educated children have spent more time in school. Therefore, they have had many experiences with waiting a longer time in order to get a reward, because waiting for rewards is fairly common in school settings.

C.   Students' choices of format may vary but should be organized in a logical manner, include the key ideas in the reading, and make use of appropriate vocabulary, as in the example on the next page.

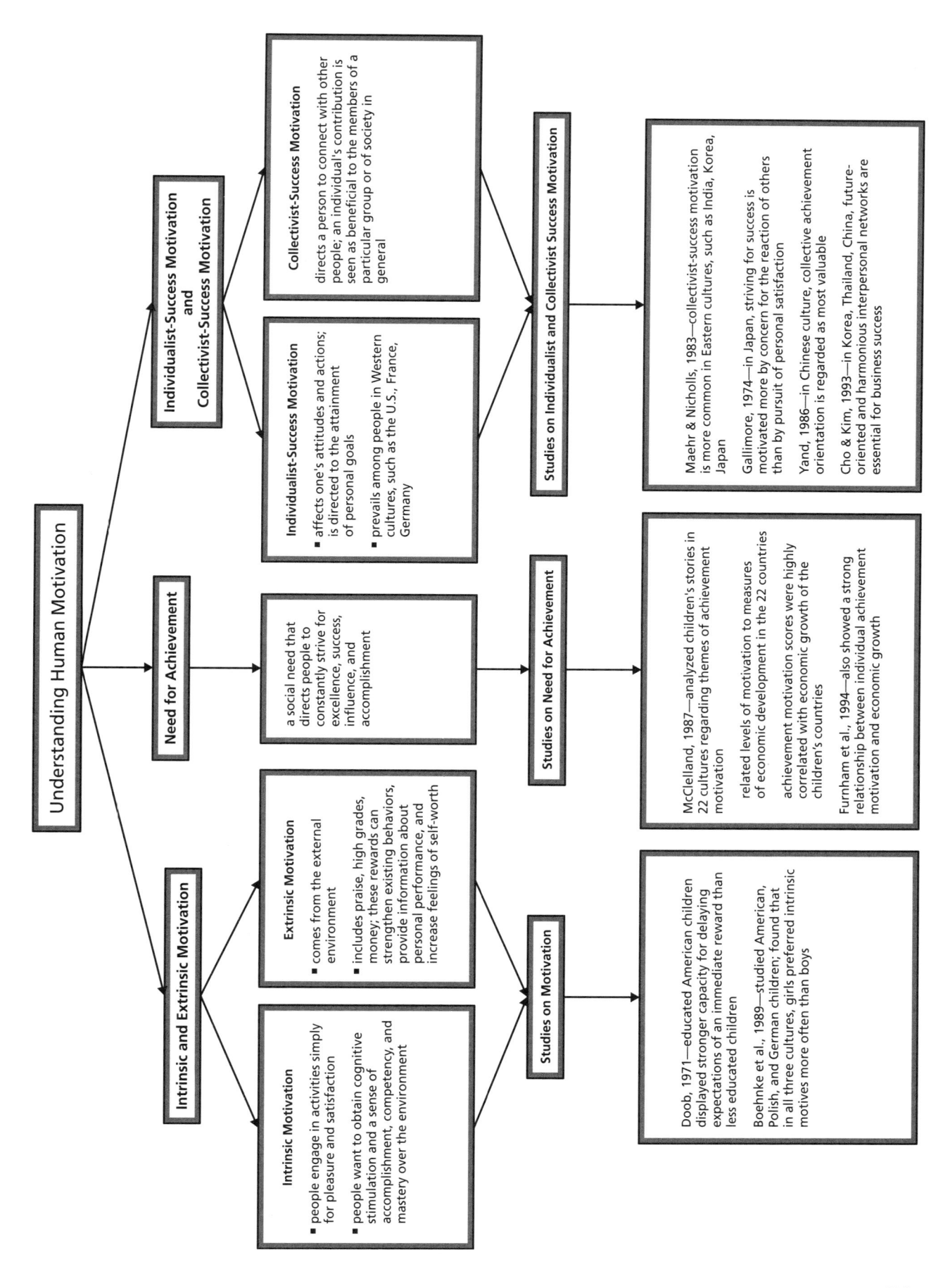

Understanding Human Motivation

Intrinsic and Extrinsic Motivation

Intrinsic Motivation
- people engage in activities simply for pleasure and satisfaction
- people want to obtain cognitive stimulation and a sense of accomplishment, competency, and mastery over the environment

Extrinsic Motivation
- comes from the external environment
- includes praise, high grades, money; these rewards can strengthen existing behaviors, provide information about personal performance, and increase feelings of self-worth

Studies on Motivation
Doob, 1971—educated American children displayed stronger capacity for delaying expectations of an immediate reward than less educated children

Boehnke et al., 1989—studied American, Polish, and German children; found that in all three cultures, girls preferred intrinsic motives more often than boys

Need for Achievement
a social need that directs people to constantly strive for excellence, success, influence, and accomplishment

Studies on Need for Achievement
McClelland, 1987—analyzed children's stories in 22 cultures regarding themes of achievement motivation

related levels of motivation to measures of economic development in the 22 countries

achievement motivation scores were highly correlated with economic growth of the children's countries

Furnham et al., 1994—also showed a strong relationship between individual achievement motivation and economic growth

Individualist-Success Motivation and Collectivist-Success Motivation

Individualist-Success Motivation
- affects one's attitudes and actions; is directed to the attainment of personal goals
- prevails among people in Western cultures, such as the U.S., France, Germany

Collectivist-Success Motivation
directs a person to connect with other people; an individual's contribution is seen as beneficial to the members of a particular group or of society in general

Studies on Individualist and Collectivist Success Motivation
Maehr & Nicholls, 1983—collectivist-success motivation is more common in Eastern cultures, such as India, Korea, Japan

Gallimore, 1974—in Japan, striving for success is motivated more by concern for the reaction of others than by pursuit of personal satisfaction

Yand, 1986—in Chinese culture, collective achievement orientation is regarded as most valuable

Cho & Kim, 1993—in Korea, Thailand, China, future-oriented and harmonious interpersonal networks are essential for business success

71

Writing about Figures

Students' writing may vary but should accurately reflect the information in the chapter and in the photographs, make use of appropriate vocabulary, and be grammatically correct.

ANSWER KEY TO THE STUDENT BOOK EXERCISES

UNIT I

Chapter 1

Activate Your Knowledge, p. 3

A. Students' work will vary. Any reasonable work is acceptable.

B. 1. a 2. b 3. a

C. Students' answers may vary. (The correct answers are 1. I 2. L 3. I 4. L 5. I 6. I 7. L 8. L 9. I)

Scanning and Skimming, p. 5

A. Headings:

Human Behavior

The Value of Behaviors

The Significance of Behavior

B. Fear of an animal is not inherited. It is something we have to learn.

C. 1 and 2. Students' predictions and questions may vary. Anything reasonable is acceptable.

Monitor Reading Comprehension, p. 7

Before You Continue Reading

a

INTRODUCTORY READING, p. 8

Before You Continue Reading

1. c 2. a

Text Analysis, p. 11

A. Explanation: Behavior helps animals escape predators, seek out mates, gain dominance over others of the same species, and respond to change in the environment.

Supporting Details: (1) Animals can run away from a predator. (2) Mate selection in animals often involves elaborate behaviors that assist them in identifying the species and sex of a potential mate.

Transition: As we will read later, animals have a variety of behaviors that allow them to exert dominance over members of the same species.

B. First Main Idea: Animal activities appear to have a purpose.

Supporting Details: (1) Birds search for food. (2) Birds take flight as you approach.

Supporting Details: (1) Squirrels collect and store nuts and acorns. (2) Squirrels "scold" you when you get too close. (3) Squirrels learn to visit sites where food is available.

Second Main Idea: Animal activities are adaptive and help the species survive.

Supporting Detail: Birds that do not take flight at the approach of another animal will be eaten by predators.

Conclusion: We need to be careful about attaching meaning to what animal do because they may not have the same thoughts and motivations we have.

C. 1. I 2. L 3. I 4. L 5. I 6. I 7. L 8. L 9. I

D. 1. The main purpose of plant and animal behavior is to enable the species to survive.

2. The value of these behaviors to the baby gull is that the baby will get food and therefore

survive. The value of these behaviors to the gull species is that babies will survive, grow up, and reproduce. They will continue the species.

3. If the baby herring gull does not peck at the red spot on the parent's bill, the parent will not regurgitate any food, and the baby gull will not have anything to eat.

Vocabulary in Context, p. 13

B. Excerpt 2: c

Excerpt 3: a

Using the Dictionary, p. 15

Excerpt 2: 1. 3b   2. c

Activate Your Knowledge, p. 16

A. 1 and 2. Students' answers may vary. Any reasonable answer is acceptable.

B. Students' work may vary. Any reasonable examples are acceptable.

C. Students' work may vary. Any reasonable definition and examples are acceptable.

Scanning and Skimming, p. 17

A. Headings:

Instinctive Behavior

Learned Behavior

Kinds of Learning

B. instinctive behavior: behavior that is inborn, automatic, and inflexible
learning: behavior that requires experience and can be changed

C. Students' answers may vary. (The correct answers for 1 are b, c, e, h, j.)

Use Font Styles to Identify and Learn Key Vocabulary, p. 19

B. 1. instinctive behavior: behavior that is inborn, automatic, and inflexible; it is automatic, preprogrammed, and genetically determined

2. learning: behavior that requires experience and can be changed

3. stimulus: some change in the internal or external environment of an organism that causes it to react

4. response: an organism's reaction to a stimulus

MAIN READING, p. 20

Before You Continue Reading

1. Instinctive behavior is automatic, but learned behavior must be learned. Instinctive behavior is inflexible, but learned behavior can be changed.

2. The major advantage of instinctive behavior is that it does not leave much to chance because it is always done correctly the first time without any previous experience.

3. The goose and the spider demonstrate behaviors that are done correctly the first time and cannot be changed in any way.

Text Analysis, p. 25

A. <u>Advantages of Instinctive Behavior:</u> It is done correctly the first time. It does not have to be learned.

<u>Examples:</u> A baby gull pecks at its parent's bill and gets food. A spider builds a web. A goose rolls one of its eggs back into its nest.

<u>Drawbacks of Instinctive Behavior:</u> It cannot be modified when a new situation arises. It cannot be stopped until the behavior is completed.

<u>Examples:</u> If an egg rolls away from a goose while it is trying to put it back in the nest, it cannot stop its behavior midstride and get the egg. A goose will roll any object into its nest, even a beer can or a baseball. If a spider's web is damaged, it must build a new one; it cannot repair the web.

B. b, c, e, h, j

C. 1. imprinting   2. insight
3. habituation   4. association

D. 1. Simple animals that live a very short time and animals whose parents do not care for them when they are born find instinctive behavior advantageous. Animals that live a short time do not have time to learn complex behaviors from other animals. Animals that do not have parents to care for them when they are born must be able to perform behaviors right away, without needing to learn them.

2. For animals that live a long time, and that live in environments that change, the ability to learn many different behaviors and to be able to modify behaviors will help them adapt and survive.

3. If we had more instinctive behaviors, we would be less flexible, we would be less able to adapt to new or changing environments, and we would be less able to learn to make or do new things.

4 and 5. Students' answers will vary. Any reasonable answer is acceptable, but it must demonstrate understanding of the information in the reading.

Vocabulary in Context, p. 27

Excerpt 1: c

Excerpt 2: b

Using the Dictionary, p. 27

Excerpt 1: 1. 3   2. c

Excerpt 2: 1. 1a   2. b

Learn and Use Word Forms, p. 29

B.   1. habituated
   2. does not respond
   3. stimuli
   4. motivation
   5. association
   6. reactions
   7. adaptive
   8. imitative
   9. modify
   10. dominance

Writing Activities, p. 31

1. Students' answers may vary somewhat but must demonstrate an understanding of the diagram. For example, students need to understand that the animals in the diagram represent similar groups of animals, not only individual species; that the proportion of instinctive behavior is highest among the simplest groups of animals; that the proportion of learned behavior is highest among the more complex groups of animals; that the degree of instinctive behavior lessens and the amount of learned behavior increases with the increasing complexity of the groups of animals.

2–4. Students' answers may vary but must be accurate and must incorporate vocabulary from the chapter.

Extension Activities, p. 32

1–3. Students' work will vary but must be accurate and must incorporate vocabulary from the chapter and from their research.

Chapter 2

Activate Your Knowledge, p. 34

Students' work will vary. Any reasonable examples are acceptable.

Scanning and Skimming, p. 35

A.   Headings:

   Integration of Instinct and Learning in Animals

   A Comparison of Instinct and Learning

B.   1. Simple animals that have short lives and little contact with their parents rely most on instinctive behavior. These include many invertebrates. More complex animals, especially birds and mammals, that have long lives and extensive contact with parents rely most on learned behavior.

   2. Responses include: Instinctive behavior is hereditary; learned behavior is not. Instinctive behavior cannot be changed; learned behavior can. Instinctive behavior is done correctly the first time; learned behavior improves with practice.

C.   1 and 2. Students' predictions and questions may vary. Anything reasonable is acceptable.

INTRODUCTORY READING, p. 36

Before You Continue Reading

c

Text Analysis, p. 38

A. Main Idea: An animal's behavior may have elements that are both instinctive and learned.

Supporting Details: (1) Song sparrows inherit the basic melody of their species' song; (2) Baby birds that were raised with no adults to imitate knew only some notes, not the normal song; (3) Refinements of the song must be learned by imitating other song sparrows.

Conclusion: The characteristics of the song sparrows' song is partly instinctive and partly learned.

B. Main Idea: Many invertebrates rely on instinct for the majority of their behavior patterns, whereas many vertebrates use a great deal of learning.

Example: honeybee

Instinctive Behavior: Most of the honeybee's behavior is instinctive.

Learned Behavior: The honeybee can learn new routes to food sources.

Example: bird

Instinctive Behavior: (1) the style of a bird's nest is instinctive; (2) food-searching behavior is probably instinctive

Learned Behavior: (1) a bird's skill in building a nest may improve with practice; (2) a bird can modify its behavior to exploit unusual food sources such as bird feeders

Transition: The following table compares instinctive behaviors and learned behaviors.

C. 1. Instinctive behavior is inherited, done correctly the first time, does not require experience or memory, and cannot be changed. Learned behavior is not inherited, requires practice and memory, and can be changed.

2. Students' answers will vary but must reflect an understanding of the topic.

D. 1. c 2. a

Vocabulary in Context, p. 39

Excerpt 1: 1. c 2. b 3. b

Excerpt 2: a

Excerpt 3: 1. a 2. b 3. c

Using the Dictionary, p. 41

1. 1. a 2. a

Activate Your Knowledge, p. 41

1–3. Students' answers may vary. Any reasonable answer is acceptable but should reflect an understanding of what students have learned so far in Chapter 1 and in the Introductory Reading in Chapter 2.

Scanning and Skimming, p. 42

A. Headings:

Types of Learned Behavior

Behavior as Part of an Animal's Ecological Niche

   Territorial Behavior

   Dominance Hierarchy

   Avoiding Periods of Scarcity

B. 1. The behaviors that are involved in securing and defending an animal's territory are called territorial behaviors.

2. Within a group, dominance hierarchy helps ensure that the most favorable genes will be passed on to the next generation. Dominance hierarchy also ensures a relatively stable social group.

C. 1 and 2. Students' predictions and questions may vary. Anything reasonable is acceptable.

MAIN READING, p. 43

Before You Continue Reading

1. c

2. insight

3. b

4. Dominance hierarchy establishes a relatively stable group of animals. Dominance hierarchy ensures that

only the most dominant animals reproduce, ensuring that the most favorable genes will be passed on to the next generation. Dominance hierarchy also enables the best adapted members of the species to survive when resources are scarce.

Use Referents to Aid in Understanding Text, p. 49

B. 1. conflict (example)

2. other individuals

3. male redwing blackbird

4. other males

5. the characteristic

Text Analysis, p. 49

A. Section Topic: Types of learned behavior

<u>Type:</u> associative learning; <u>Explanation:</u> a way of learning where a sound, smell, or other stimulus becomes associated with something else <u>Example:</u> We associate the sound of a siren with the approach of an emergency vehicle.

<u>Type:</u> imprinting; <u>Definition:</u> a type of learning that takes place at a critical period in life, usually shortly after birth, that is preprogrammed and cannot be unlearned <u>Example:</u> Infants bond with their mothers. Language development of children may also be a form of imprinting.

<u>Type:</u> insight; <u>Explanation:</u> a type of learning that involves memory, a concept of self, and an ability to reorganize information <u>Example:</u> We are able to use past experiences, stored in our brains, to provide clues to solving new problems.

B. 1. Newborns grasp with their hands and feet. When a newborn's face is touched, it turns its head and begins sucking movements.

2. Students' answers will vary. Answers may include that we learn by having something explained to us, by having something shown to us, or by reading about how to do something.

3. Children learn the language spoken by the people around them through all types of learning: association (learning to associate objects with words), imprinting, and insight.

C. 1. b 2. c 3. b

D. 1. Students' answers may vary but should reflect what the students have learned in the chapter.

2. Students' answers may vary but should make sense given the author's definition of *thinking*. Most animals probably cannot think.

3. Students' answers may vary somewhat, but a conclusion may be that as children we learn whatever languages are spoken around us through imprinting, so we use one part of our brain that may involve more instinct. As adults, we learn new languages in a different way, probably through association and insight, so we use a different part of our brain for these types of learning.

4. Students' answers may vary but should reflect what they have learned so far; for example, humans live long lives and live in complex environments that require us to have the ability to solve problems and to modify our behavior to meet changing situations.

5. a and b. Students' answers may vary. Males probably have red shoulder patches so they can recognize other males of the same species, and chase them out of their territory. Females do not need red shoulder patches because they do not appear to defend territory, and it would not be an advantage for a male to attack a female.

Vocabulary in Context, p. 52

Excerpt 1: 1. b 2. a

Excerpt 2: 1. a 2. a 3. b

Using the Dictionary, p. 53

Excerpt 1: 1. 2b   2. c

Excerpt 2: 1. 2a (2b is also acceptable) 2. b

Learn and Use Word Forms, p. 54

B. 1. visualize
2. modifications
3. allocate
4. does not reproduce
5. dominant
6. exploit
7. associative
8. Imitative
9. stimuli
10. refinements

Writing Activities, p. 56

1–3. Students' answers may vary but must be accurate and must incorporate vocabulary from the chapter.

Extension Activities, p. 56

1–4. Students' work will vary but must be accurate and must incorporate vocabulary from the chapter and from their research.

UNIT 2

Chapter 3

Activate Your Knowledge, p. 61

A. Students' work will vary. Any reasonable characteristics and examples are acceptable.

Scanning and Skimming, p. 62

A.

```
┌─────────────────────────┐
│  The Concept of Culture │
└───────────┬─────────────┘
     How can we define culture?
            ▼
┌──────────────────────────────────────────┐
│ Defining culture is very difficult because│
│ it is so complex. Cultural behavior       │
│ involves several characteristics that     │
│ distinguish it from noncultural behavior. │
└──────────────────────────────────────────┘
```

- It must involve concepts, generalizations, abstractions, and ideas.
- In a culture, learning is active; information is shared. Information is transmitted from one organism to another.
- Culture is learned from others.
- A culture has concrete and abstract artifacts.

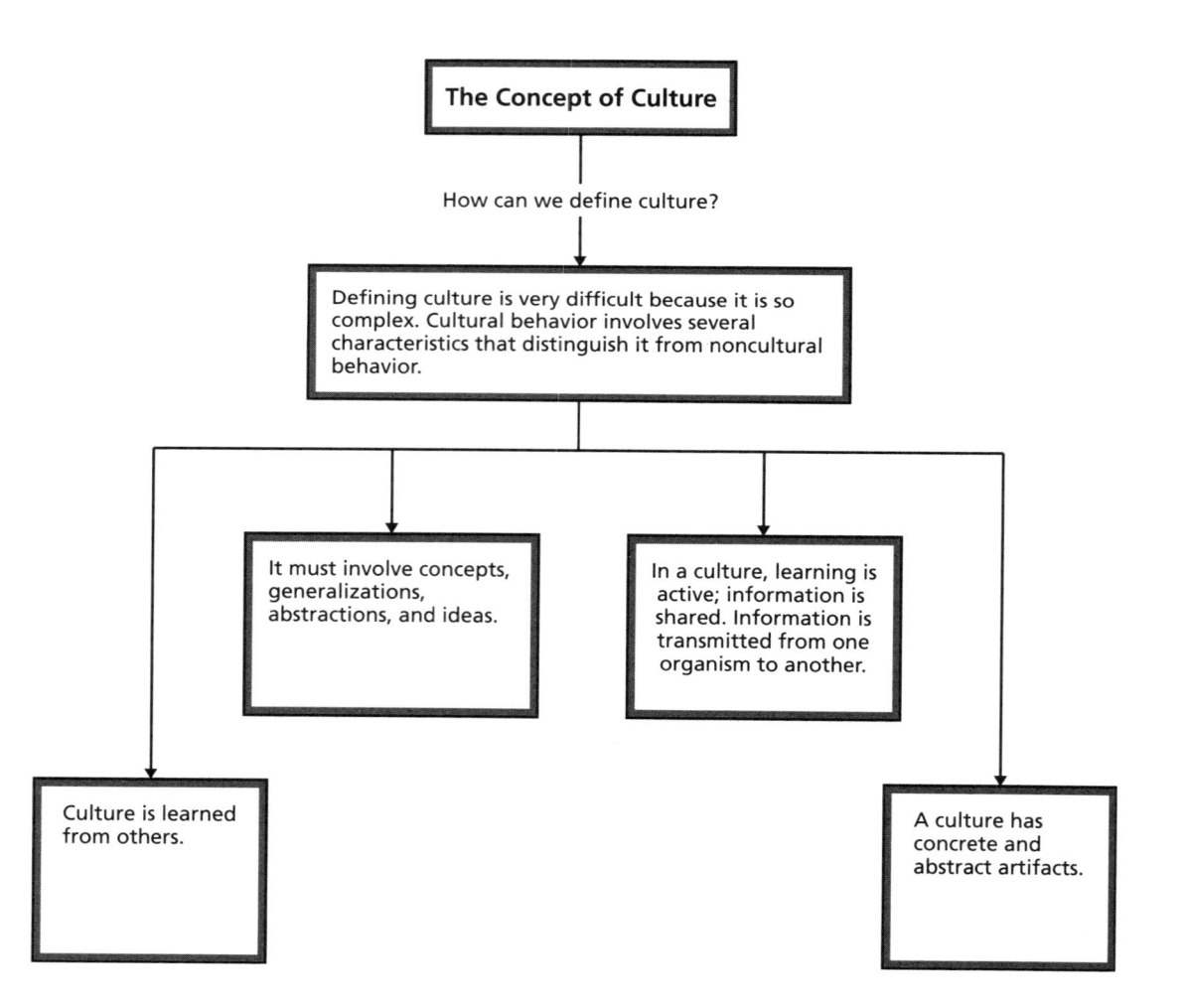

B. 1 and 2. Students' predictions and questions may vary. Anything reasonable is acceptable.

Annotate Text, p. 63

B. Refer to the annotation in paragraph 8.

INTRODUCTORY READING, p. 64

Before You Continue Reading

1. a   2. c

Text Analysis, p. 68

B. <u>Characteristic:</u> Cultural behavior involves concepts, generalizations, abstractions, and ideas.

<u>Noncultural Behavior:</u> Ants cannot make any adjustments to their nest-building behavior. It is not part of a concept.

<u>Cultural Behavior:</u> The author's wall building involved concepts, general ideas, and problem solving.

<u>Characteristic:</u> Cultural behavior is transmitted extragenetically from one organism to another.

<u>Noncultural Behavior:</u> The ants' nest-building information is solely genetic.

<u>Cultural Behavior:</u> The author's wall-building information was shared extragenetically.

<u>Characteristic:</u> Cultures have artifacts—intentionally made objects.

<u>Noncultural Behavior:</u> The ants' nest is a natural, instinctively made object.

<u>Cultural Behavior:</u> The tools and books the author used to help him make his wall, and the wall itself, are artifacts.

C. 1. Students' answers will vary somewhat but should reflect the information in the reading. The ants' nest is an example of noncultural behavior, whereas the author's wall building is an example of cultural behavior. The ants' nest building is preprogrammed (instinctive), the information is not shared extragenetically, the nest cannot be modified in any way through generalizations or ideas, and the nest is a natural object, not something made intentionally. In contrast, the author learned to build his wall through shared information and learning. The wall was made intentionally. It can be modified.

2. Singing is genetic. Songs are learned.

3 and 4. Students' answers will vary but must reflect understanding of the information presented in the chapter.

Sentence Focus, p. 69

B. Paragraph 8: a

Paragraph 10: a

Vocabulary in Context, p. 71

Paragraph 5: 1. a   2. b

Paragraph 9: 1. a   2. c

Using the Dictionary, p. 71

1. 1a   2. a

Activate Your Knowledge, p. 72

A. Students' work may vary. Anything is acceptable but should reflect an understanding of what students have learned so far.

Scanning and Skimming, p. 73

A. Headings:

The Concept of World View

Religious Beliefs as Part of a Culture's World View

The Religious Concepts of Polytheism and Monotheism

Aspects of the American World View

B. 1. World view is a set of assumptions about the way things are. World view is the collective interpretation of and response to the natural and cultural words in which a society of people live.

2. When people codify their world view, they talk about, share, and pass on their assumptions about the way things are.

C. 1 and 2. Students' predictions and questions may vary. Anything reasonable is acceptable.

MAIN READING, p. 74

Before You Continue Reading

1. b   2. a   3. b

Text Analysis, p. 81

A.

1. biological humans

↓

2. possible behavior patterns

↓

[funnel] ← the group's collective interpretation and response to its natural and cultural environments ← 3. a group's natural and cultural environments

4. a culture's world view

↓

5. a specific cultural system

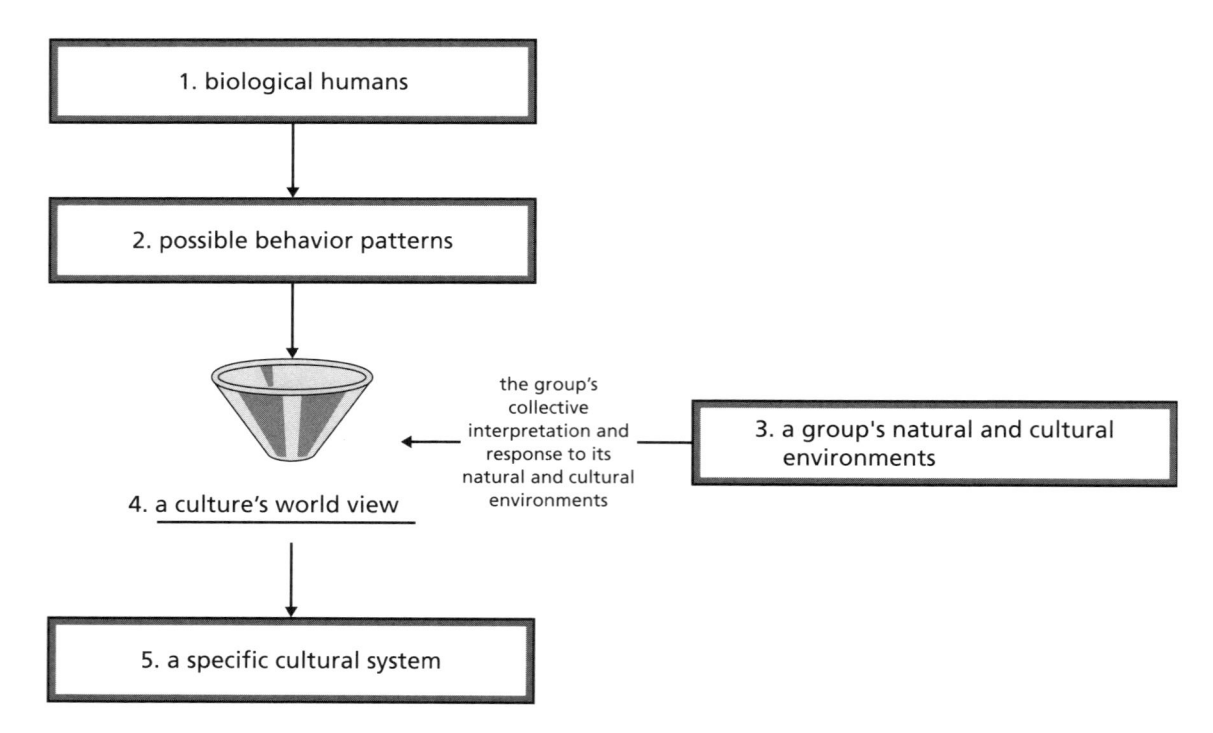

B. 1. the peoples of the American Arctic

2. the author and the readers

3. the use of the term *Eskimo*

C. 1. Some factors that help to account for cultural variations among groups of people are the natural environment the groups live in, how the groups develop ways to cope with their environment, how their cultural system got to be the way it is, their cultural system at any point in time, and their interactions with other peoples.

2. Some factors that might cause a cultural group's world view to change include changes in the group's environment, changes in their understandings of the world around them, changes in their ability to understand and control the world around them, and encounters with other peoples.

3. The Netsilik believe that the natural world is not under their control, but under the control of the spirit world. They survive in their difficult environment by developing rules about how to treat spirits (souls), including the souls of the animals they hunt and kill. If they treat the animals' souls with respect, the animals will allow themselves to be caught, and the Netsilik will have successful hunting.

4. If a cultural group develops a sense of understanding and controlling the world, it will tend to change its religious beliefs from polytheism to monotheism.

5. According to the author, religion is one aspect of a group's cultural system. The function of religion is to allow people to codify their world view. Religion allows people to talk about, share, and pass on their assumptions about

how the world was created, about how they were created, about the way things are, and about rules of behavior.

Sentence Focus, p. 82

Paragraph 8: 1. b   2. a   3. b

Vocabulary in Context, p. 83

Paragraph 1: c

Paragraph 2: a

Paragraph 7: c

Using the Dictionary, p. 84

Excerpt 1: 1. 1   2. a

Learn and Use Word Forms, p. 85

B. 1. interacts
    2. variations
    3. adapt
    4. characteristic
    5. inventive
    6. express
    7. generalizations
    8. realization
    9. do not conceptualize
    10. transmission
    11. do not interpret
    12. stimuli (OR stimulus)

Writing Activities, p. 87

1–3. Students' answers may vary but must be accurate and must incorporate vocabulary from the chapter.

Extension Activities, p. 87

1–4. Students' work will vary but must be accurate and must incorporate vocabulary from the chapter and from their research.

Chapter 4

Activate Your Knowledge, p. 89

Students' lists will vary. Any reasonable list of traits is acceptable.

Scanning and Skimming, p. 90

A. Headings:

Religion and Religious Systems

Differences in Religious Expression among Cultures

B. 1. All religions include belief in the supernatural.

2. One religious difference among cultures is which phenomena are dealt with by religion and which phenomena are dealt with using scientific knowledge.

C. 1 and 2. Students' predictions and questions may vary. Anything reasonable is acceptable.

Monitor Reading Comprehension, p. 90

Before You Continue Reading

b

Recognizing Definitions, p. 91

1. supernatural: a force or power of being that is outside the known laws of nature

2. shaman: a person who specializes in taking care of the religious knowledge and welfare of the people in a cultural group. Shamans are part-time specialists and are usually only called on in times of crises such as an illness.

3. priest: a person who specializes in taking care of the religious knowledge and welfare of the people in a cultural group. Priests are full-time specialists who train for their profession, learning what is passed down by their predecessors.

INTRODUCTORY READING, p. 92

Text Analysis, p. 95

A. *See diagram on the next page.*

Text Analysis, p. 95

A.

Differences in Religious Expression among Cultures

Belief in the Supernatural

type: monotheism
- **reasons:**
  - the group has gained distinct control over its habitat
  - the influence of the gods is less direct because scientific knowledge is more important to the group
- **example of a society:** the early agriculturalists of Southwest Asia

type: polytheism
- **reasons:**
  - people interact with their environments on a personal level
  - the group tends not to have a political system with formal leadership
  - people see themselves as one of many natural phenomena
- **example of a society:** the Eskimo

Specialists

shaman
- **power:**
  - power comes directly from the supernatural
  - shamans are chosen for the position
  - shamans have real supernatural power
  - they are needed only in special situations such as curing illness
- **type of society:**
  - egalitarian or less complex horticultural societies that have no full-time specialists in anything
  - religious knowledge is known and practiced by everyone

priest
- **power:**
  - they are the holders of religious knowledge
  - priests are trained for their profession
  - priests have knowledge of the supernatural
  - priests may also have political power
- **type of society:** more complex cultures

B. 1. monotheistic and polytheistic religions
2. societies like the Eskimo
3. societies like the Eskimo

C. 1. M 2. M 3. P 4. P

D. 1. The supernatural is a force or power of being that is outside the known laws of nature.
2. Two common needs among all people are personal survival and having a world view.
3. Shamans are part-time specialists; priests are full-time. Shamans receive power from the supernatural, and they tell the supernatural what to do on our behalf. Priests have knowledge of the supernatural, and tell us what to do on behalf of the supernatural. Shamans do not have any special political power, but priests may have considerable political power.
4. Priests have sometimes gained political power because in some cultures the political system and its leaders are hard to separate from the religious system and its leaders.

Sentence Focus, p. 97

B. 1. a 2. b

Vocabulary in Context, p. 97

Paragraph 2: 1. b 2. a

Paragraph 7: a

Using the Dictionary, p. 98

Excerpt 1: 1. 4 2. d

Excerpt 2: a

Activate Your Knowledge, p. 99

1–2. Students' lists may vary. Any reasonable answer is acceptable but should reflect some understanding of what students have learned so far.

Recognizing Definitions, p. 99

1. world view: the collective interpretation and response of a people to their natural and cultural environment
2. syncretism: the act of incorporating new beliefs into existing beliefs to produce a synthesis
3. stimulus diffusion: the stimulus for an invention diffuses into a culture from another culture, even if the invention itself does not

Scanning and Skimming, p. 100

A. and B. Process: discovery

Definition: the realization and understanding of some set of relationships; discovery is knowledge

Examples: Answers will vary depending on the cultures students choose. The examples should match with the process and definition.

Process: invention

Definition: the creation of abstract or concrete artifacts that put a discovery to use; invention involves application of a discovery

Examples: Answers will vary depending on the cultures students choose. The examples should match with the process and definition.

Process: diffusion

Definition: the giving and taking of culture among different societies

Examples: Answers will vary depending on the cultures students choose. The examples should match with the process and definition.

Process: acculturation

Definition: rapid diffusion under the influence of a dominant society

Examples: Answers will vary depending on the cultures students choose. The examples should match with the process and definition.

Process: revolution

Definition: a radical change in aspects of a society, except for its government

Examples: Answers will vary depending on the cultures students choose. The examples should match with the process and definition.

D. 1 and 2. Students' predictions and questions may vary. Anything reasonable is acceptable.

MAIN READING, p. 101

Before You Continue Reading

1. The topic is culture change, and the main idea is that all cultures change, although they may change slowly or rapidly.

2. The topic is the related processes of discovery and invention as means of culture change, and the main idea is that discovery is new knowledge that may or may not be accepted or applied as an invention.

3. The topic is diffusion as a means of culture change, and the main idea is that different societies always give and take culture among themselves, although they do not always borrow everything that could be borrowed, or if they do borrow ideas and technologies, they often adapt them.

Text Analysis, p. 105

A. <u>Examples of discovery:</u> the nature of fire; the discovery that the earth was not the center of the universe

<u>Examples of invention:</u> using fire for cooking, light, heat, and scaring away animals; making fire by striking flint with another rock or by rubbing two pieces of wood together; the wheel; the telescope; using the telescope to keep track of merchant vessels in Venice

<u>Examples of diffusion:</u> clothing styles; fast-food restaurants; religious beliefs

<u>Examples of acculturation:</u> the acculturation of Native Americans into European-based society; the acculturation of European Christians in Islamic Spain; the cargo cults in some South Pacific island societies

<u>Examples of revolution:</u> a scientific revolution

B. 1. a process of culture change
   2. acculturation
   3. acculturation by force and with violence

C. 1. c 2. a

D. 1. Discovery refers to new knowledge. Invention refers to the application of the new knowledge.

2. A discovery or invention might not be accepted by a particular culture because it does not fit the culture's existing system. For example, it might not be needed, or it may be inconsistent with some aspect of the culture's system such as its religious beliefs.

3. Some factors that help determine whether cultural diffusion takes place are the culture's perceived need for a given idea or technology, or the unacceptable nature of the new idea or technology.

4. Acculturation may take place voluntarily, or it may take place by force and with violence.

5. a. Galileo's telescope was used to observe the movements of the sun, the moon, the planets, and other objects in the universe. It was also used for business purposes, to keep track of the merchant vessels that came into and left the port of Venice.

   b. Only the business use was acceptable in the culture of his time because the scientific observations were in conflict with the culture's religious beliefs.

6. Sequoyah's invented alphabetic system represents an example of stimulus diffusion because Seqouyah took an artifact—the writing system for English—and adapted it to create a new writing system for the Cherokee language. He did not adopt the English writing system intact.

Sentence Focus, p. 109

B. a

C. Usually thought of in the context of violent overthrow of an existing government—as in the American, French, and Russian revolutions—<u>a revolution</u> <u>can</u> also <u>refer</u> to a radical change in other aspects of society.

D. 1. c 2. c 3. b

Vocabulary in Context, p. 110

Paragraph 2: a

Paragraph 3: c

Paragraph 5: 1. a 2. b

Using the Dictionary, p. 110

Excerpt 1: 1. 1a(1) 2. is the act of putting a discovery to use

Excerpt 2: 1. 4 2. the diffusion of discoveries and artifacts, i.e., the giving and taking of culture among different societies

Learn and Use Word Forms, p. 112

B. 1. intervene 6. is incorporated
2. applicable 7. adoption
3. variations 8. modifications
4. acculturated 9. contact
5. stimuli 10. expression

Writing Activities, p. 114

1–3. Students' answers may vary but must be accurate and must incorporate vocabulary from the chapter.

Extension Activities, p. 114

1–5. Students' work will vary but must be accurate and must incorporate vocabulary from the chapter and from their research.

UNIT 3

Chapter 5

Activate Your Knowledge, p. 119

B. Students' answers will vary. (The correct answers are 2, 3, 5, 7.)

D. The Dark Ages are also known as the Middle Ages. When: 476–1000 A.D. Where: Europe What: a time during which civilization experienced a decline. Students' work for additional ideas or information will vary.

Scanning and Skimming, p. 121

A. Headings:

Aristotle's Beliefs

Aristotle's Ideas during the Dark Ages

The Seventeenth-Century Scientific Revolution

B. 1. c 2. b 3. c

C. 1 and 2. Students' predictions and questions may vary. Anything reasonable is acceptable.

INTRODUCTORY READING, P. 123

Before You Continue Reading

The topic of the first four paragraphs is Aristotle's ideas, and the main idea is that Aristotle was an ancient Greek philosopher and teacher whose scientific beliefs were taught, forgotten, then reintroduced to Europe, where they eventually became part of Christian doctrine.

Text Analysis, p. 126

B.

II. The scientific revolution was the opening of a new era in European history.

A. Opening a new era

1. European thinkers had come against the limits of ancient knowledge.

2. The certainties of the past were called into question because there were too many contradictions between theory and observation.

C. 2, 3, 5, 7

D. 1. People believed that the Earth stood still and that the Sun revolved around the Earth because they did not feel the Earth move, and they saw that the Sun seemed to revolve around the Earth.

2. Mathematics, experimentation, and deduction were needed to understand that the Sun is at the center of our solar system and that the Earth revolves around the Sun.

3. When the new science emerged, people relied on observation and experimentation to understand the world.

4. The new science was termed a "scientific revolution" because it challenged thousands of years of beliefs and certainty about the nature of the universe, and because it challenged common sense, that is, what people could see and feel.

Answer Key to the Student Book Exercises 85

Sentence Focus, p. 128

A. Paragraph 2: 1. c 2. a 3. c 4. a

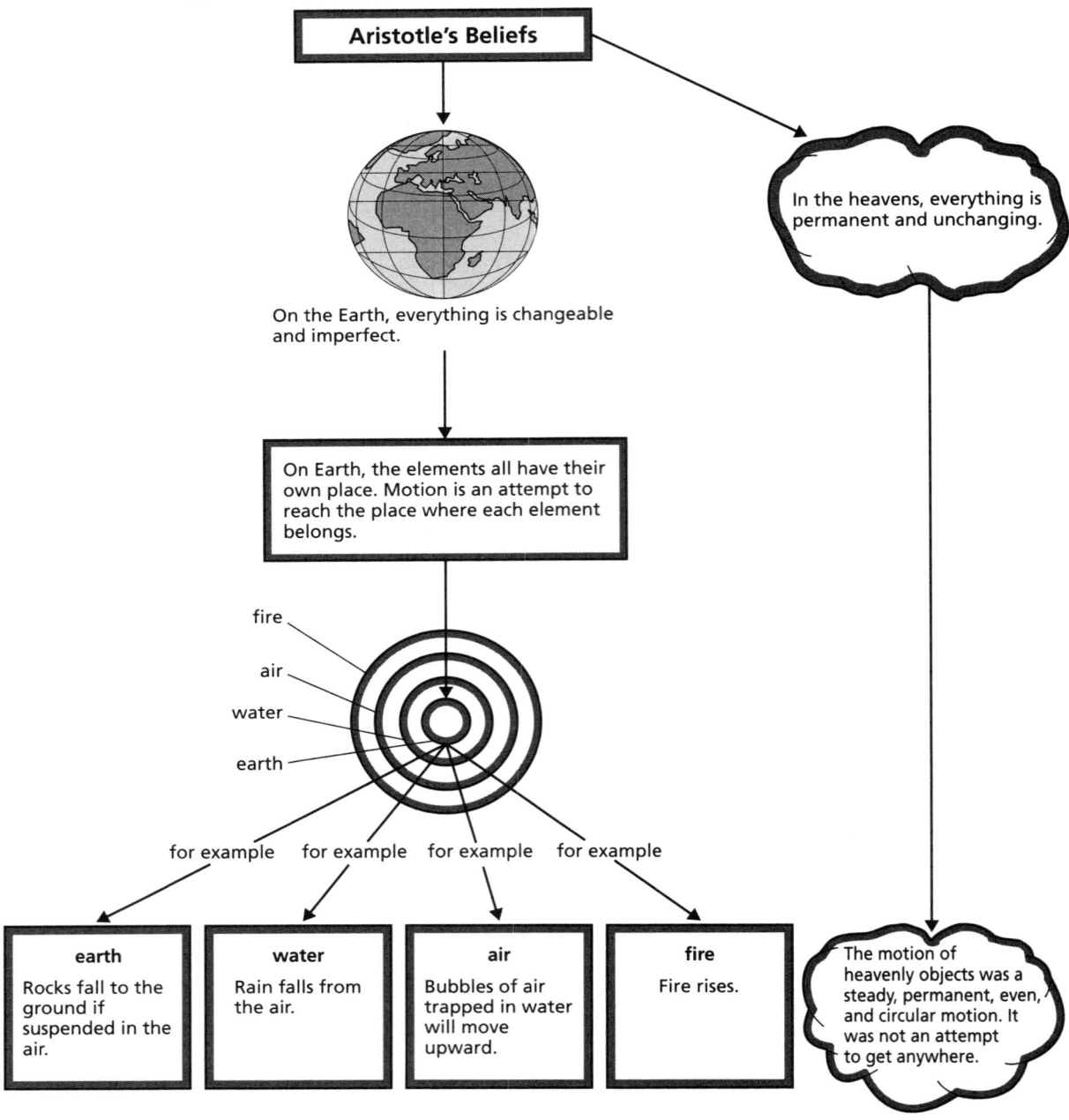

B.

```
                    Aristotle's Beliefs
                    /              \
                   ↓                ↓
        On the Earth, everything    In the heavens, everything is
        is changeable and           permanent and unchanging.
        imperfect.
                   ↓                        ↓
        On Earth, the elements all have     The motion of heavenly
        their own place. Motion is an       objects was a steady,
        attempt to reach the place where    permanent, even, and
        each element belongs.               circular motion. It was
                                            not an attempt to get
                                            anywhere.
```

Concentric circles labeled (from outside in): fire, air, water, earth

for example / for example / for example / for example

earth	water	air	fire
Rocks fall to the ground if suspended in the air.	Rain falls from the air.	Bubbles of air trapped in water will move upward.	Fire rises.

Vocabulary in Context, p. 130

Paragraph 1: 1. end 2. classify
Paragraph 3: c
Paragraph 4: 1. a 2. stopped
Paragraph 5: 1. b 2. c 3. looking through a telescope

Using the Dictionary, p. 131

Excerpt: 1. the Church's system of beliefs

2. introduced

Write a Summary, p. 131

In the seventeenth century, a new science emerged which was based on mathematics, experimentation, and deduction, and which challenged people's most basic assumptions and beliefs about the nature of the universe.

Activate Your Knowledge, p. 132

1 and 2. Students' answers may vary. Any reasonable answer is acceptable but should reflect an understanding of what students have learned so far. For example, the students should know that before the Scientific Revolution, people believed the Earth was in the center of the universe, that the Earth stood still, and that the sunrevolved around the Earth.

Scanning and Skimming, p. 133

A. Headings:
   The European Contribution
   Heavenly Revolutions
   Problems with Aristotle's Universe
   Nicolaus Copernicus

B. 1. One advantage was that Aristotle incorporated a view of the physical world that coincided with a view of the spiritual and moral one. Another advantage was that it was easily incorporated into Christian doctrine.

   2. One of the problems was that it could not explain why the seasons were not perfectly equal, or why the planets looked closer or farther away, brighter or darker, at different times of the year.

C. 1 and 2. Students' predictions and questions may vary. Anything reasonable is acceptable.

MAIN READING, p. 134

Before You Continue Reading

1. The topic of these two paragraphs is the essential characteristics of the new science, and the main idea is that the main contributions in astronomy, modern chemistry, anatomy, biology, and physics were European.

2. The topic of this paragraph is Aristotle's view of the world, and the main idea is that his world view fit with a view of the spiritual and moral world that were also part of Christian doctrine.

3. The topic of this paragraph is the problems with Aristotle's explanation of the universe, and the main idea is that the solution to these problems, although it answered some questions, was very complicated.

Text Analysis, p. 137

A. <u>Characteristic:</u> materialistic

   <u>Realization:</u> The universe is composed of matter in motion.

   <u>Explanation:</u> The stars and planets were made of the same matter that was found on earth.

   <u>Characteristic:</u> mathematical

   <u>Realization:</u> Calculation has to replace common sense as the basis for understanding the universe.

   <u>Explanation:</u> Scientific experimentation included measuring repeatable phenomena.

B. 1. Learning through common sense involved only what people could observe through their senses, whereas learning through mathematics, experimentation, and deduction involved going beyond observable phenomena and sometimes challenging common sense.

   2. a. People could not see or feel the Earth move; therefore, it wasn't moving.

      b. The use of common sense can be thought of as representing associative learning because people associate perceived lack of motion as true lack of motion. The use of common sense to conclude that something that does not appear to be moving is, therefore, not moving, can also be considered a fundamental form of insight, because insight involves drawing on past experiences and problem solving.

Answer Key to the Student Book Exercises *87*

3. The use of mathematics, experimentation, and deduction represents learning through insight in a more complex way than the use of common sense does. Scientists drew on past experiences in an entirely new way to come up with new solutions to problems.

4. Copernicus revised Aristotle's explanations of planetary motion by stating that the sun, not the Earth, was at the center of the universe, and as a consequence, he simplified the explanations of planetary motion.

5. One result of Copernicus's work was that people were slightly better able to predict the position of the planets. Another result is that other astronomers began to make new calculations.

C.

The nature of the universe

<u>What Aristotle Had Taught:</u> The stars and planets were made of some perfect ethereal (abstract) substance.

<u>The Problems with Aristotle's Belief:</u> They would not be subject to the same rules of motion as earthly objects, and so their motions were difficult to predict.

The center of the universe

<u>What Aristotle Had Taught:</u> The Earth was at the center of the universe, and the sun, the moon, and the planets revolved around it in a perfect circle.

<u>The Problems with Aristotle's Belief:</u> The seasons were not equal; the planets looked closer or farther away and brighter or darker at different times of the year.

The difference between the Earth and the rest of the universe

<u>What Aristotle Had Taught:</u> The sun, moon, and planets were all perfect spheres, whereas the Earth was imperfect.

<u>The Problems with Aristotle's Belief:</u> It required a very complex system of 55 epicycles and of eccentric circles to explain the motion of the sun, the moon, and the planets.

Sentence Focus, p. 139

1. a   2. b

Vocabulary in Context, p. 140

Paragraph 1: 1. made of   2. substance

Paragraph 3: b

Paragraph 4: 1. a   2. c

Using the Dictionary, p. 140

Excerpt 1: 1. 2b   2. c

Excerpt 2: 1. 2   2. b   3. b

Write a Summary, p. 142

Students' summaries will vary somewhat but should include the main ideas. A sample summary is as follows:

> The new science was based on the understanding that the universe is composed of matter in motion and that calculation and experimentation needed to replace common sense in order to understand the universe. Aristotle's view of the universe supported Christian doctrine, but it could not explain observable phenomena such as the movement of the stars and planets. Copernicus's belief that the sun, not the earth, was the center of the universe solved many of the problems caused by Aristotle's teachings and stimulated other astronomers in their work.

Learn and Use Word Forms, p. 142

B. 1. predicted
    2. contributor
    3. contradicted
    4. dominated
    5. observations
    6. system
    7. modified
    8. hypotheses
    9. astonished
    10. revolved (OR revolves)
    11. Experimentation

Writing Activities, p. 144

1–3. Students' answers may vary but must be accurate and must incorporate vocabulary from the chapter.

Extension Activities, p. 145

1–4. Students' work will vary but must be accurate and must incorporate vocabulary from the chapter and from their research.

Chapter 6

Activate Your Knowledge, p. 147

A. and **B.** Students' work will vary. Any reasonable descriptions are acceptable.

C. Students' answers may vary, but students should note that the detailed photos disprove Aristotle's theory that the moon and sun are perfect, unblemished, unchanging spheres.

Scanning and Skimming, p. 148

A. Headings:

The Telescope

Observations of the Moon's Surface

B. 1. Galileo observed the moon through his telescope.

2. He observed that the moon's surface is not smooth, uniform, and precisely spherical; rather, it is uneven, rough, and full of cavities and prominences.

C. 1 and 2. Students' predictions and questions may vary. Anything reasonable is acceptable.

INTRODUCTORY READING, p. 149

Before You Continue Reading

The topic of this section by Galileo is the telescope, and the main idea is that Galileo built his own telescope and made observations of the moon with it.

Text Analysis, p. 152

A. Students' flow charts may vary. An example is as follows:

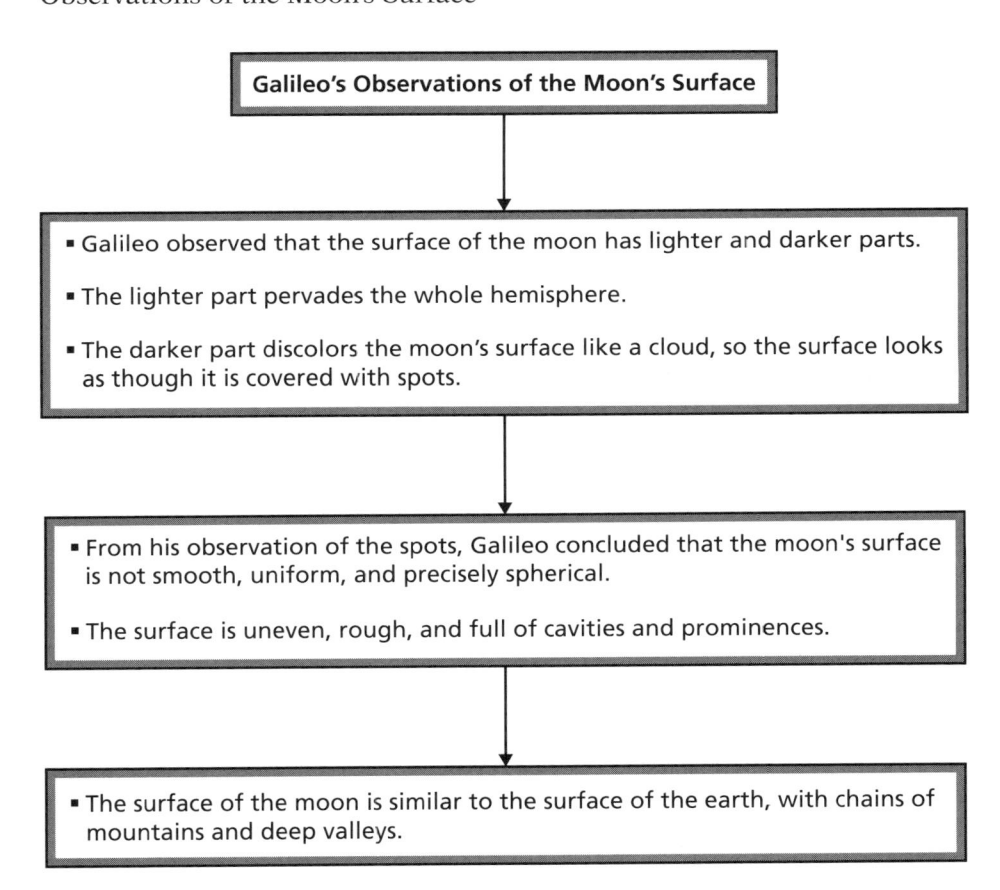

```
┌─────────────────────────────────────────────┐
│   Galileo's Observations of the Moon's Surface   │
└─────────────────────────────────────────────┘
                       │
                       ▼
┌─────────────────────────────────────────────────────────────┐
│ • Galileo observed that the surface of the moon has lighter │
│   and darker parts.                                          │
│ • The lighter part pervades the whole hemisphere.            │
│ • The darker part discolors the moon's surface like a cloud, │
│   so the surface looks as though it is covered with spots.   │
└─────────────────────────────────────────────────────────────┘
                       │
                       ▼
┌─────────────────────────────────────────────────────────────┐
│ • From his observation of the spots, Galileo concluded that  │
│   the moon's surface is not smooth, uniform, and precisely   │
│   spherical.                                                 │
│ • The surface is uneven, rough, and full of cavities and     │
│   prominences.                                               │
└─────────────────────────────────────────────────────────────┘
                       │
                       ▼
┌─────────────────────────────────────────────────────────────┐
│ • The surface of the moon is similar to the surface of the   │
│   earth, with chains of mountains and deep valleys.          │
└─────────────────────────────────────────────────────────────┘
```

B. 1. No, he wasn't. Galileo heard that a Fleming had made a telescope, and after Jacques Badovere confirmed this report, Galileo made his own telescope.

2. Before Galileo's observations, people believed that the moon's surface was perfect, unblemished, and spherical.

3. Galileo observed that the moon's surface was uneven and rough. His observations changed people's beliefs because he proved that celestial objects were not perfect as people had believed.

Sentence Focus, p. 152

4. look close

5. reports were told

6. which some people believed

7. try very hard

8. find out how

9. make

10. clearly saw things look big and close

Vocabulary in Context, p. 153

Paragraph 2: 1. telescope   2. a

Paragraph 3: 1. b   2. the sun and the moon; of the Earth

Using the Dictionary, p. 154

Excerpt 1: 1. 1b   2. a

Excerpt 2: 1. 1   2. a

Write a Summary, p. 155

Students' summaries will vary somewhat but should include the main ideas. A sample summary is as follows:

> Galileo Galilei made major contributions to the Scientific Revolution, in part by popularizing Copernicus's work, and through his scientific observations. He was the first person to use a telescope to observe heavenly objects, and his observations of the moon proved that it was like the Earth, and not a smooth, perfect sphere.

Activate Your Knowledge, p. 155

C. 1. Newton's first law

2. Newton's third law

3. Newton's second law

4. Newton's third law

5. Newton's first law

6. Newton's second law

Scanning and Skimming, p. 157

A. Headings:

Tycho Brahe and Johannes Kepler

Galileo Galilei

Sir Isaac Newton

Newton's Three Laws of Motion

B. 1. Tycho Brahe discovered a nova.

2. Johannes Kepler discovered that planets orbited the sun in an elliptical path, not a circular path.

3. Sir Isaac Newton answered the question, "What is motion?"

C. Headings:

Galileo's Early Work

Galileo's Conflict with the Church

Galileo's Trial

D. 1. Aristotle's scientific beliefs were part of official Church doctrine.

2. Church doctrine was that everything in the universe revolved around the Earth, and that celestial objects were different from the Earth. Galileo believed that moons revolved around other objects in the universe, and that celestial objects such as the moon were similar to the Earth.

3. Galileo was more interested in advocating a new view of the universe. He did not want to challenge the Church.

E. 1 and 2. Students' predictions and questions may vary. Anything reasonable is acceptable.

MAIN READING, p. 158

Before You Continue Reading

1. The topic of paragraphs 2 and 3 is the discoveries of scientists such as Tycho Brahe and Johannes Kepler, and the main idea is that their discoveries disproved Aristotelian teachings.

2. The topic of paragraphs 4 and 5 is Galileo, and the main idea is that his discoveries popularized Copernicus's heliocentric theory but resulted in his being condemned by the Church.

3. The topic of paragraphs 6–8 is Sir Isaac Newton's work, and the main idea is that his laws of motion joined together Kepler's and Galileo's work, thus completing the world of the new science.

4. The topic of paragraphs 9–13 is Galileo's early work, and the main idea is that his experiments and publications often got him in trouble with his colleagues and with the Church.

5. The topic of paragraphs 14–16 is Galileo's conflict with the Church, and the main idea is that his published dialogue was seen as a criticism of Church doctrine and resulted in his being investigated by the Jesuits.

Text Analysis, p. 166

B. *See diagram below.*

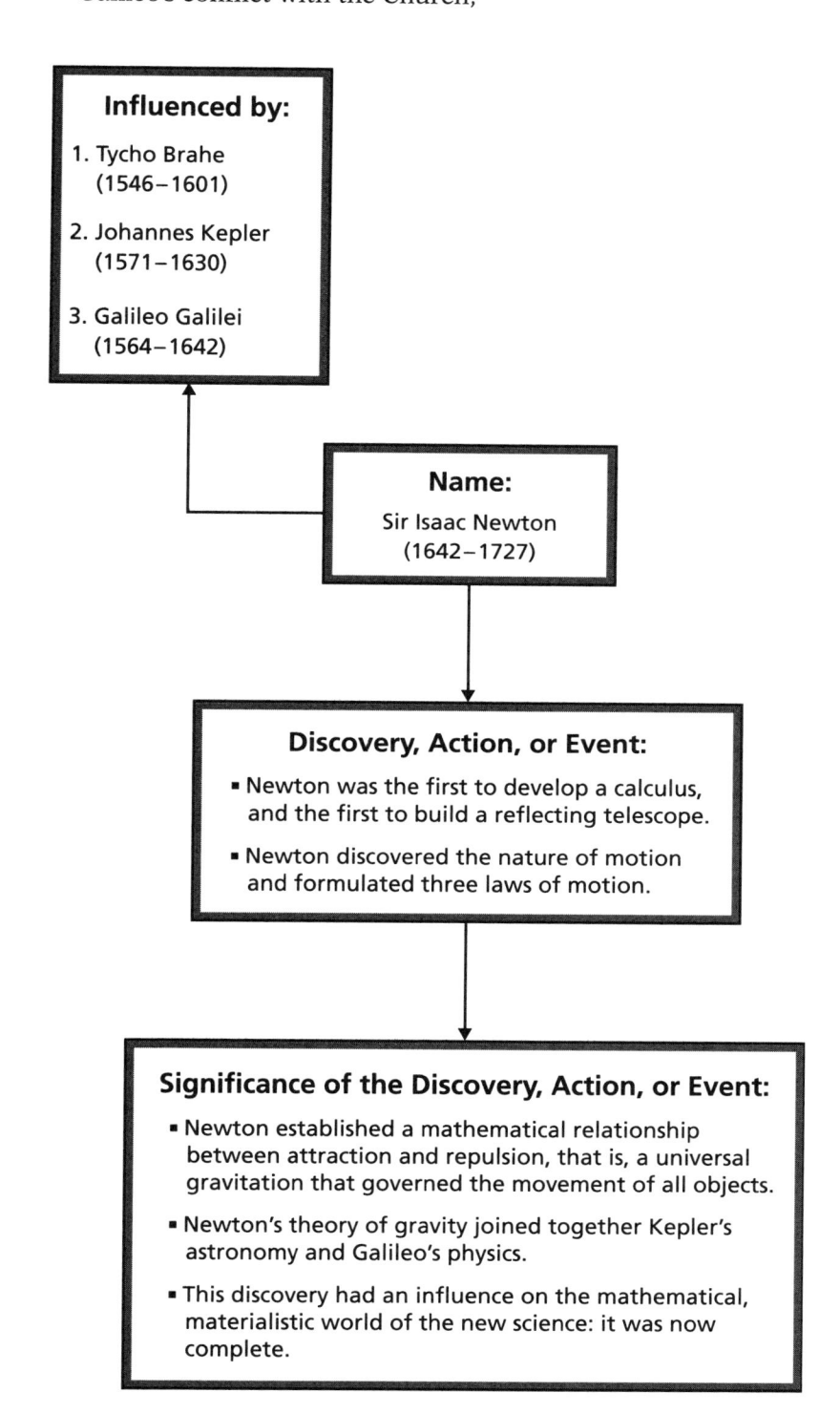

Influenced by:

1. Tycho Brahe (1546–1601)
2. Johannes Kepler (1571–1630)
3. Galileo Galilei (1564–1642)

Name:

Sir Isaac Newton (1642–1727)

Discovery, Action, or Event:

- Newton was the first to develop a calculus, and the first to build a reflecting telescope.
- Newton discovered the nature of motion and formulated three laws of motion.

Significance of the Discovery, Action, or Event:

- Newton established a mathematical relationship between attraction and repulsion, that is, a universal gravitation that governed the movement of all objects.
- Newton's theory of gravity joined together Kepler's astronomy and Galileo's physics.
- This discovery had an influence on the mathematical, materialistic world of the new science: it was now complete.

C. 1. Copernicus's main contribution to the new science was his heliocentric view of the universe.

2. If moons revolved around Jupiter, then clearly not all heavenly bodies revolved around the Earth.

3. Galileo's discoveries of moons revolving around Jupiter and the imperfect surface of the moon disproved the Church's doctrine that everything in the universe revolved around the Earth, and that everything in the universe was perfect. In other words, his discoveries proved that the Church was wrong, and in the historical context of the day, this was unacceptable to the Church.

Sentence Focus, p. 167

Reason for paragraph 6 question: stimulate the reader's curiosity

Reason for title of second passage: stimulate the reader's curiosity

Reason for paragraph 14 questions: make a transition to the next paragraph

Reason for paragraph 17 question: help the reader understand a problem or side of a controversy

Vocabulary in Context, p. 168

Paragraph 1: revolve

Paragraph 2: 1. a brightly burning star 2. unchanging 3. c

Paragraph 3: a

Paragraph 6: c

Paragraph 10: c

Using the Dictionary, p. 169

Excerpt: Students' answers will vary somewhat. An example is as follows:

> According to the Church, in making public his experiments and discoveries, Galileo supported heliocentrism. As a result, Galileo committed the crime of heresy, which means he held opinions that were contrary to Church dogma, or doctrine. Because of this, the Inquisition, which was the official Church tribunal for discovering and punishing acts of heresy, charged Galileo with heresy and tried him for this crime. He was convicted and had to renounce his belief that the Earth moves. Galileo's punishment was to spend the rest of his life under house arrest.

Write a Summary, p. 170

Students' summaries will vary somewhat but should include the main ideas. A sample summary is as follows:

> The new science began when European scientists used observations, mathematical calculations, and logical deductions. Aristotelian teachings were disproved through Tycho Brahe's discovery of a nova, Johannes Kepler's discovery of the elliptical orbits of planets, and Galileo's discovery of four moons of Jupiter. Sir Isaac Newton formulated laws of motion and of gravity, thus demonstrating that the universe, like the Earth, is composed of matter in motion. When Galileo popularized Copernicus's heliocentric theory, and especially after he published his *Dialogue*, he was seen as challenging Church doctrine, which eventually resulted in his being tried by the Inquisition and condemned by the Church.

Learn and Use Word Forms, p. 170

B. 1. formulated
2. rejected
3. did not challenge
4. supportive
5. orbit
6. reaction
7. compiled
8. revealed
9. debatable
10. interpreting

Writing Activities, p. 172

1–3. Students' answers may vary but must be accurate and must incorporate vocabulary from the chapter.

Extension Activities, p. 173

1–3. Students' work will vary but must be accurate and must incorporate vocabulary from the chapter and from their research.

UNIT 4

Chapter 7

Activate Your Knowledge, p. 177

1 and 2. Students' work will vary. Any reasonable examples are acceptable. For number 2, students should be able to see that fifteenth-century artists used Greek fluted columns and Roman arches.

Scanning and Skimming, p. 178

A. Headings:

Artists in Ancient Greece and Rome

Artists in the Middle Ages

Artists in the Renaissance

The Idea of a Renaissance

B. 1. Artists were regarded as working in a manual profession.

2. Artists were regarded as working in a manual profession.

3. Artists were regarded as educated professionals, and had a new social status.

C. 1 and 2. Students' predictions and questions may vary. Anything reasonable is acceptable.

Recognize and Understand the Passive Voice, p. 179

Virtually all cultures, ancient or modern, nurtured specialists who design and/or embellish everday items or materials used in ritual. Whether Hopi, African, Mesoamerican, European, or Asian, these men and women were highly skilled workers. Sometimes those who were considered best at such expression were recognized as "artists" and were elevated in their society to a high level of regard; in some cultures they were encouraged to sign their works. Although not all these creators are recognized as artists, the visual arts—grand or modest, public or private, religious or secular—are a regular feature of human culture, and those who create these works are fundamental to most societies. Individuals in some cultures, for example fifth-century China and fifteenth-century Italy, began to write down their aesthetic aspirations and deeply held values as expressed in the visual arts.

1. b   2. c   3. c

INTRODUCTORY READING, P. 180

Before You Continue Reading

1. The topic of paragraphs 1 and 2 is artists in virtually all cultures, and the main idea is that they were considered highly skilled workers with manual skills.

2. The topic of paragraphs 3 and 4 is artists in Ancient Greece and Rome and in the Middle Ages in the West, and the main idea is that all these cultures viewed art as a manual profession.

Text Analysis, p. 182

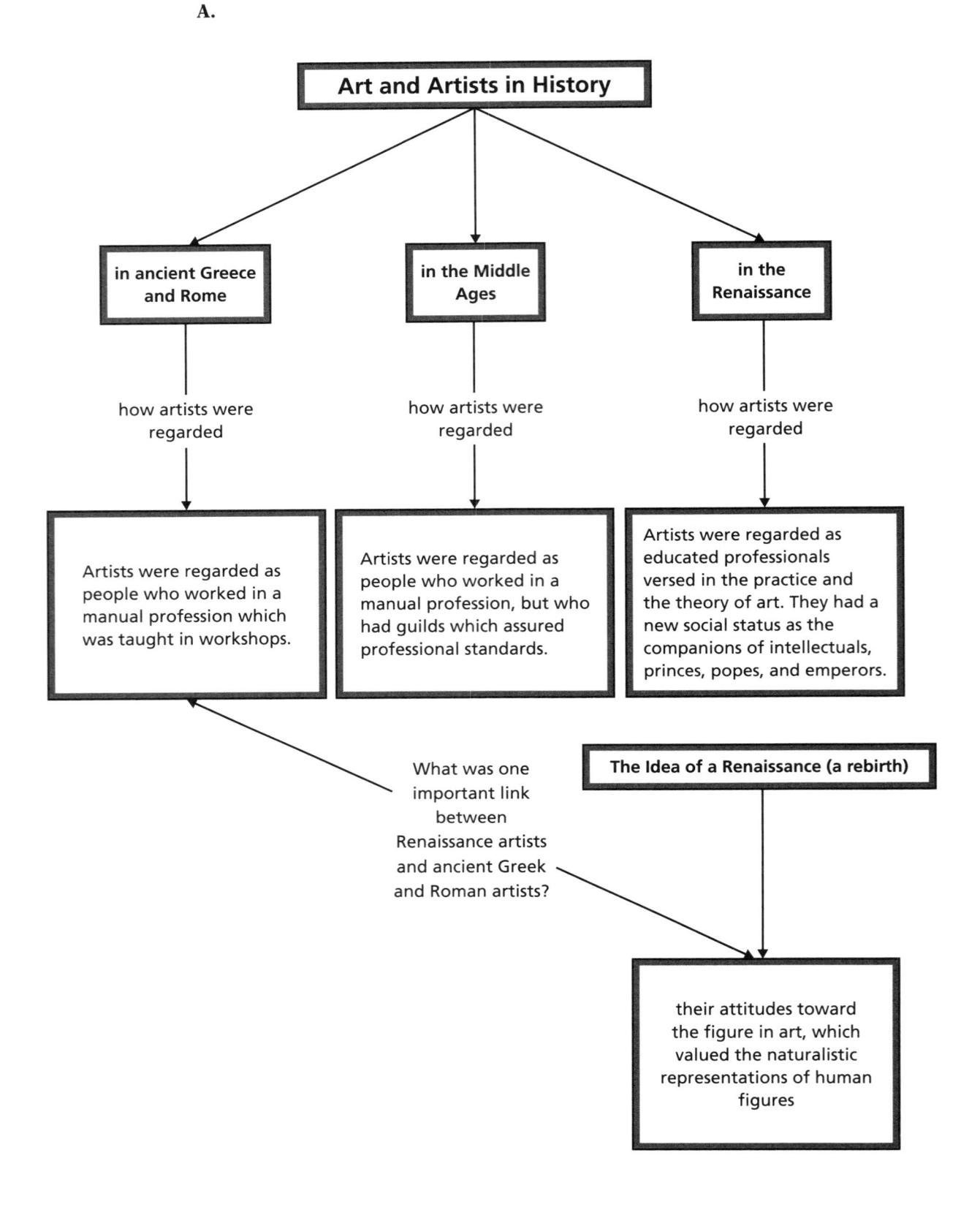

A.

```
                    ┌─────────────────────────┐
                    │  Art and Artists in History │
                    └─────────────────────────┘
                          │        │        │
         ┌────────────────┘        │        └────────────────┐
         ▼                         ▼                         ▼
┌──────────────────┐    ┌──────────────────┐      ┌──────────────────┐
│ in ancient Greece│    │ in the Middle    │      │ in the           │
│ and Rome         │    │ Ages             │      │ Renaissance      │
└──────────────────┘    └──────────────────┘      └──────────────────┘
         │                       │                          │
  how artists were        how artists were           how artists were
     regarded                regarded                   regarded
         ▼                       ▼                          ▼
```

- **in ancient Greece and Rome** — how artists were regarded: Artists were regarded as people who worked in a manual profession which was taught in workshops.

- **in the Middle Ages** — how artists were regarded: Artists were regarded as people who worked in a manual profession, but who had guilds which assured professional standards.

- **in the Renaissance** — how artists were regarded: Artists were regarded as educated professionals versed in the practice and the theory of art. They had a new social status as the companions of intellectuals, princes, popes, and emperors.

What was one important link between Renaissance artists and ancient Greek and Roman artists?

The Idea of a Renaissance (a rebirth)

their attitudes toward the figure in art, which valued the naturalistic representations of human figures

B. 1. The manual arts referred to practical handicrafts and occupations, whereas the liberal arts referred to mathematics, grammar, philosophy, and logic.

2. Guilds are legal organizations similar to trade unions. They ensure standards within a field.

3. In the Renaissance, artists were seen as educated professionals, people who understood both the practice and the theory of art. In the Middle Ages, in contrast, artists were seen as people who had a craft, people who were professionals in a manual trade.

4. As artists and writers started to emphasize the scientific and intellectual aspects of art, the status of artists began to change. Artists were seen as needing mathematics to study proportion and geometry to calculate perspective.

5. The Renaissance is considered a "rebirth" because at the time people had a renewed interest in classical Greek and Roman art, and adapted these aesthetics to the art of their own time.

Sentence Focus, p. 184

The traditional classification of the Western visual arts as manual, or mechanical, arts **was transformed** in the fourteenth and fifteenth centuries. Both artists and writers began to emphasize the scientific and intellectual aspects of art, often incorporating the liberal arts into the education of artists. It **was argued** that mathematics, for example, was necessary for the study of proportion, and that geometry figured in the calculation of perspective. The artist was beginning to **be seen** as an educated professional versed in both the practice and the theory of art. This attitude that the artist had to be a skilled and educated individual **was accompanied** by a new social status: artists became the companions of intellectuals, princes, popes, and emperors.

1. b   2. a   3. c

Vocabulary in Context, p. 185

Paragraph 1: b
Paragraph 5: a
Paragraph 6: 1. a   2. c   3. b
Paragraph 7: a

Using the Dictionary, p. 186

Excerpt: a

Write a Summary, p. 186

Students' summaries will vary somewhat but should include the main ideas. A sample summary is as follows:

> Virtually all cultures have had artists, although the way artists were viewed has varied across time and place. In ancient Greece and Rome and in the West during the Middle Ages, art was thought of as a manual profession. However, in the Renaissance, as artists began to emphasize the importance of mathematics and geometry to art, people began to view the artist as an educated professional, and the artist's social status changed. The idea of a Renaissance came about in the fifteenth century as people gained a renewed interest in the art of antiquity, which provided stimulation for artistic change.

Activate Your Knowledge, p. 187

A. 1 and 2. Students' answers may vary. Any reasonable answer is acceptable but should reflect an understanding of what students have learned so far. For instance, in number 1, students should know that proportion and perspective were not used in the painting in Figure 7.2, but were used in the painting in Figure 7.3. In number 2, students should point out that artists had better social status and socialized with important people such as princes, popes, and emperors.

Scanning and Skimming, p. 188

A.

I. Italian Renaissance Humanism
II. The Fifteenth-Century Artist in Europe

Answer Key to the Student Book Exercises 95

    A. Changing Patterns of Patronage in Europe

    B. The Significance of Perspective

    C. Masaccio's Great Work

III. The Renaissance in Flanders
Flemish Painting: The Limbourg Brothers

B. 1 and 2. Students' predictions and questions may vary. Anything reasonable is acceptable.

MAIN READING, p. 190

Before You Continue Reading

1. The topic of paragraphs 1 and 2 is Florence, and the main idea is that Florence was an independent republic which was dominated for a long time by the Medici family.

2. The topic of paragraph 3 is humanism, and the main idea is that it inspired much Renaissance art.

3. The topic of paragraphs 4–6 is the fifteenth-century European artist, and the main idea is that artists were viewed as trained intellectuals, and they received support from religious and secular patrons.

4. The topic of paragraphs 7–9 is perspective, and the main idea is that perspective was an important innovation in Renaissance art and is clearly represented in Masaccio's work, *The Trinity*.

Text Analysis, p. 196

A. <u>three-dimensional figures:</u> d and e, donors; a, God the Father; c, St. John; f, Virgin Mary: <u>Significance of the elements:</u> The donors comprise the base of the triangle; God the Father forms the apex, or peak, of the triangle; the significance of Saint John and the Virgin Mary is not mentioned.

    g, illusionary space: <u>Significance of the illusionary space:</u> It provides clarity and helps create the triangle as a unifying compositional form.

B. 1. Humanist attitudes about the self made artists as individuals more important. Artists began to be viewed as trained intellectuals who were familiar with the classics and with geometry.

2. Patronage of the arts became important to the wealthy middle class, who commissioned many works of art, especially for their private homes.

3. The most important innovations in Renaissance art were the use of proportion and perspective.

4. Unlike the Italians, Flemish artists were not very interested in the art of antiquity. They were more interested in painting everyday scenes such as landscapes.

Sentence Focus, p. 198

Students' summaries will vary somewhat but should all include changing the passive voice to the active voice, and should be a paraphrasing of the paragraph. The following summary is an example:

> In the Renaissance, a number of disciplines formed the basis of humanism. These disciplines came from ancient Greek and Latin texts, which had inspired the intellectuals of the time. The wealthy especially liked the concepts of pride and fame, and these ideas were the basis for the design of such works as Leonardo Bruni's tomb.

Vocabulary in Context, p. 199

Paragraph 4: c

Paragraph 5: b

Paragraph 6: a

Using the Dictionary, p. 199

Excerpt 1: 1. 1b (from *patron* definition) 2. d

Excerpt 2: 1. 1a 2. c

Write a Summary, p. 201

Students' summaries will vary somewhat but should include the main ideas. A sample summary is as follows:

> During the fifteenth century, Florence and Flanders were centers of Renaissance art. Humanism

inspired much Renaissance art in at least two ways. First, the concepts of pride and fame led to a new view of the artist as an individual, and of all individuals as appropriate subjects of artistic works. Artists were viewed as trained intellectuals, and they received support from religious and secular patrons, who commissioned works for their private homes and for their tombs. Perspective was an important innovation in Renaissance art and is clearly represented in Masaccio's work, *The Trinity*. In contrast to Italian artists, who took classical Greek and Roman subjects and styles as important artistic subjects, Renaissance artists in Flanders tended to focus on everday scenes with everyday people, such as landscapes and farmers.

Learn and Use Word Forms, p. 201

B. 1. recede

2. commission

3. representations

4. modeled

5. demonstrated

6. inspiring

7. incorporation

8. supporters

9. reproductions

10. composition

Writing Activities, p. 203

1–3. Students' answers may vary but must be accurate and must incorporate vocabulary from the chapter.

Extension Activities, p. 204

1–4. Students' work will vary but must be accurate and must incorporate vocabulary from the chapter and from their research.

Chapter 8

Activate Your Knowledge, p. 206

1–3. Students' answers will vary. Any reasonable answers are acceptable. In item 1, students should see that all three illustrations include writing.

Scanning and Skimming, p. 207

A. Headings:

Chinese Aesthetic Theory

The Six Canons of Painting

B. 1. Their highest aim was to capture the spirit of what was depicted, not just its appearance.

2. Students' answers will vary.

C. 1 and 2. Students' predictions and questions may vary. Anything reasonable is acceptable.

INTRODUCTORY READING, P. 208

Before You Continue Reading

The topic of paragraphs 1 and 2 is China's aesthetic theory, and the main idea is that in Chinese painting, which derives from the art of writing, both the act of painting and the picture carry important meaning.

Text Analysis, p. 210

A. <u>Xie He</u>: century: sixth; title of his work: *Gu hua pin lu (Classified Record of Ancient Painters)*; format: a treatise comprising six canons of painting; summary of ideas: A painting must have spirit, be structurally sound, faithfully portray forms and color, be properly planned, and transmit knowledge of past painting traditions; significance: judges painters and paintings.

<u>Ching Hao</u>: century: tenth; title of his work: *Record of Brush Methods*, or *Essay on Landscape Painting*; format: a narrative essay; summary of ideas: His essay presents six essentials of painting, which are spirit, rhythm, thought, scenery, brush, and ink, and it describes the difference between resemblance and truth, or spirit; significance: lays down the concept of painting and its expression.

B. 1. Chinese art includes writing because it derives from the concept of writing as an art.

2. The *dao* influenced Chinese painting by inspiring artists to view their paintings in a holistic way, and to view idea and technique as one.

3. The three major points in the Six Canons of Painting are the importance of considering the concept of *qi*, or cosmic spirit, faithfulness to form and color, and reverence for tradition, in all of an artist's work.

Sentence Focus, p. 211

Pair 1: a

Pair 2: d

Pair 3: c

Vocabulary in Context, p. 212

Paragraph 1: 1. c   2. b   3. a   4. a, c, e, f

Paragraph 2: a

Paragraphs 3 and 4: 1. c   2. a

Using the Dictionary, p. 212

Excerpt 1: 1. 4b   2. c

Excerpt 2: 1. 3   2. a, b, c, d

Write a Summary, p. 214

Students' summaries will vary somewhat but should include the main ideas. A sample summary is as follows:

> China has a very old painting tradition, which is based on the art of writing. According to Chinese aesthetic theory, artists must capture not only the technique of painting, but also the spirit of painting. Xie He in the sixth century and Ching Hao in the tenth century wrote formal essays in which they describe the ideals of painting and ways to judge both artists and their work.

Activate Your Knowledge, p. 214

Students' answers may vary. Any reasonable answer is acceptable but should reflect an understanding of what students have learned so far in Unit 4 and in the Introductory Reading in Chapter 8.

Scanning and Skimming, p. 215

A.

I. The Artist Li Cheng (919–967)

II. Realism in Chinese Art

III. Landscape Painting during the Tenth–Twelfth Centuries

IV. Later Landscape Painters

B. 1. Li Cheng was such an important Chinese artist because he was considered the ideal Chinese painter.

2. The primary aim of realism in Chinese landscape art is natural appearance.

C. 1 and 2. Students' predictions and questions may vary. Anything reasonable is acceptable.

MAIN READING, p. 216

Before You Continue Reading

1. The topic of paragraphs 1–3 is the art of Li Cheng, and the main idea is that as one of China's ideal painters, he probably influenced many other painters to follow his style of monochrome paintings of landscapes.

2. The topic of paragraphs 4 and 5 is realism in Chinese art, and the main idea is that the Chinese painter's approach to realism included attempting a natural appearance and the use of shifting perspective.

3. The topic of paragraphs 6–8 is tenth–twelfth-century Chinese landscape painting, and the main idea is that during this time Chinese dynasties supported artists through academies of painting and through other forms of patronage, and influenced the development of landscape painting styles.

Text Analysis, p. 221

A. *Buddhist Temple in the Hills after Rain*

Elements of the Painting: autumn skies, low valleys, mountain pathways, bent and twisted trees, a group of huts, two pavilions built over water; buildings and figures are painted in great detail; the temple in the center is parallel to the mountain peaks in the distance.

Significance of the Elements: The brush strokes describe the sharp outlines of the trees and buildings; the brush strokes create a sense of dimension in the painting, so that the bridge in the foreground looks close to the viewer, the pavilion looks farther away, and the mountains in the background look more distant; this is a good example of shifting perspective; the symmetrical configurations of mountains and water are associated with the grand, ordered, and powerful tenth-century Chinese empire; in the composition, nature is revealed as if the viewer were really walking out-of-doors; the purpose of the painting is to provide spiritual solace and refreshment.

Early Spring

Elements of the Painting: A poem is written at the top; rocks and trees are painted in the foreground, and mountains and trees are painted in the background.

Significance of the Elements: The poem at the top is an example of calligraphy as well as literature; the poem could be the artist's interpretation of the painting; the painting is an example of shifting perspective, where the rocks and trees in the foreground look closer, whereas the stream on the left and the mountains in the background look farther away; the viewer can also examine the general structure of nature and small details.

B. 1. Li Cheng is such an important figure in the history of Chinese art because his work represents the ideal as described in the Six Canons of Painting, and because it exemplifies the use of shifting perspective, which is an important component of realism in Chinese art.

2. Tenth-century Chinese landscape art can be characterized as somewhat realistic because it aims for truth to natural appearance and demonstrates shifting perspective. It can also be characterized as a visual exercise, because the viewer visually moves through the painting, examining it as a whole and in detail.

3. Landscape artists were supported through the publication of books which helped them study art, through patronage by emperors, and through art academies.

4. The author implies that during the Song dynasty, the Chinese experienced a rebirth of their literature, because the author says that the Song dynasty was characterized by a return to older Chinese sources and of intellectual activity with regard to poetry, history, and especially philosophy.

5. We can understand that Confucius's teachings encouraged people to be virtuous, to accept their responsibilities to society and to the state, and to follow an ethical code in their conduct.

Sentence Focus, p. 222

Students' answers will vary. Possible answers are: viewers, travelers, hikers, observers, wanderers, people

Vocabulary in Context, p. 223

Paragraph 4: b

Paragraphs 8 and 9: a

Using the Dictionary, p. 223

Excerpt 1: 1. 2 2. a

Excerpt 2: 1. 1 2. c

Write a Summary, p. 224

Students' summaries will vary somewhat but should include the main ideas. A sample summary is as follows:

Chinese landscape art, which has a long history, is characterized by the use of monochrome ink, and is closely associated with calligraphy. In fact, many landscape paintings include writing such as poems. Chinese landscape painting is also characterized by realism through shifting perspective, and usually invites the viewer to travel through the painting, both as a visual exercise and to gain spiritual nourishment. In the tenth through twelfth centuries, and in later times as well, landscape painters received considerable support from emperors.

Learn and Use Word Forms, p. 225

B. 1. influential

2. composition

3. revealed

4. nurtured

5. representative
6. reverence
7. depictions
8. commissions
9. preference
10. modeled
11. support

Writing Activities, p. 227

1–3. Students' answers may vary but must be accurate and must incorporate vocabulary from the chapter.

Extension Activities, p. 227

1–4. Students' work will vary but must be accurate and must incorporate vocabulary from the chapter and from their research.

UNIT 5

Chapter 9

Activate Your Knowledge, p. 231

1. Students should know from Chapter 3 that the main characteristics of cultural behavior are that it is learned, it is transmitted from one person to another, and from one generation to the next, but not through genetics; cultural behavior involves concepts, generalizations, abstractions, and ideas; cultural behavior includes the presence of both abstract and concrete artifacts.

2. Students' answers may vary, but students should realize that within any cultural group, individual members will not all think alike, and may even think quite differently from each other. In cultures that value individualism, people will certainly think differently.

Scanning and Skimming, p. 232

A. Headings:

The Concept of Psychological Universals

Basic Definitions: Culture

Characteristics of Cultures

B. cross-cultural psychology: the critical and comparative study of cultural effects on human psychology

psychological universals: phenomena that are common for people in several, many, or even all cultures

culture: a set of attitudes, behaviors, and symbols shared by a large group of people, and usually communicated from one generation to the next

explicit characteristics: overt customs, observable practices, and typical behavioral responses

implicit characteristics: the organizing principles that are inferred to lie behind the explicit behaviors

C. 1 and 2. Students' predictions and questions may vary. Anything reasonable is acceptable.

INTRODUCTORY READING, P. 233

Before You Continue Reading

1. The topic of paragraphs 1–3 is cross-cultural psychology, and the main idea is that the aim of cross-cultural psychology is to study how culture affects human psychology and how this is similar and different among different cultures.

2. The topic of paragraphs 4 and 5 is psychological universals, and the main idea is that there may be human traits such as personality characteristics that are the same across all cultures.

3. The topic of paragraphs 6 and 7 is culture, and the main idea is that the concept of culture has many definitions, but a specific one will be used in this chapter.

Text Analysis, p. 236

A. Students' work will vary depending on the formats they chose to use in organizing paragraphs 7 and 8. A sample is as follows:

```
                              ┌─────────┐
                              │ Culture │
                              └────┬────┘
                         ┌─────────┴─────────┐
                         ▼                   ▼
```

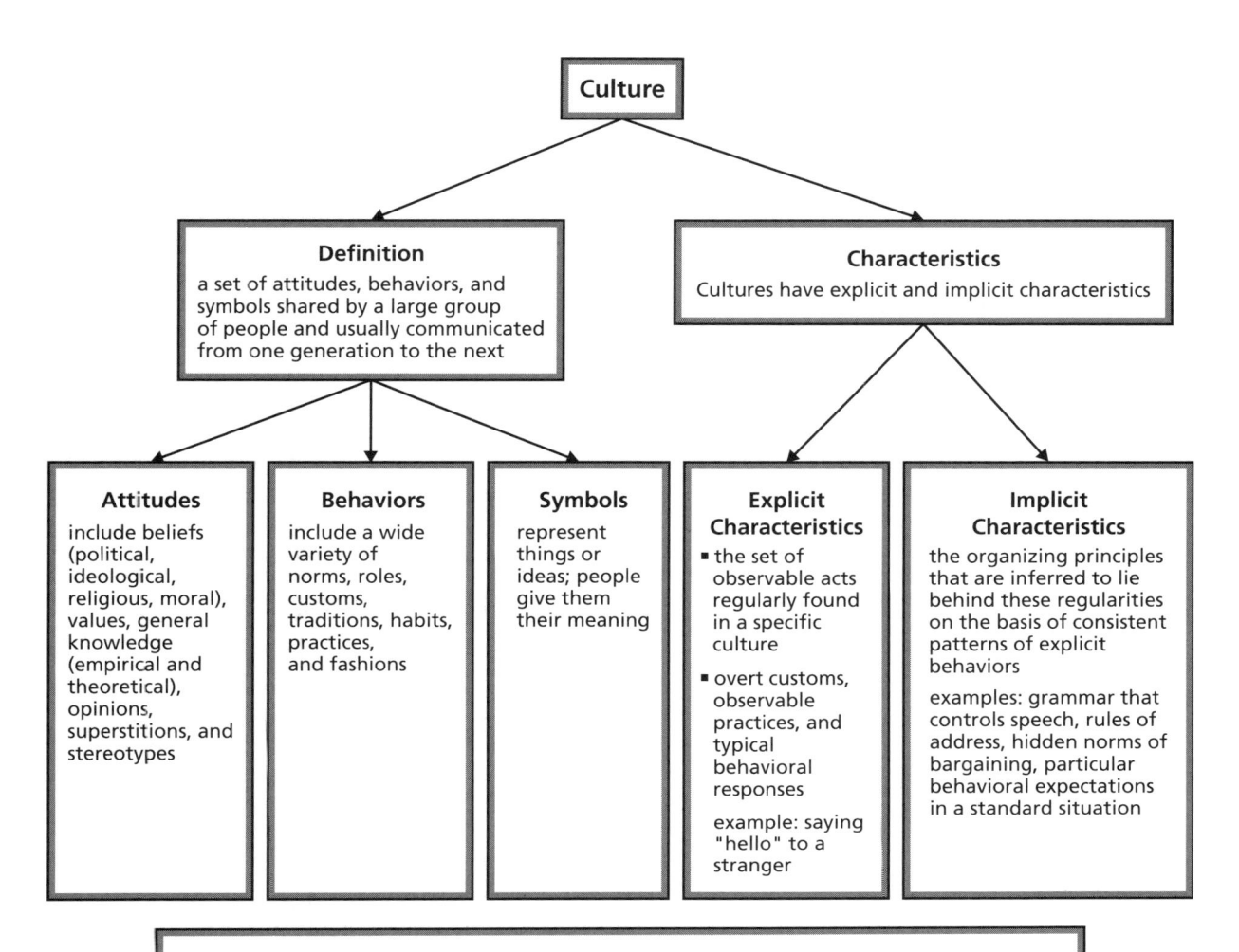

Definition	Characteristics
a set of attitudes, behaviors, and symbols shared by a large group of people and usually communicated from one generation to the next	Cultures have explicit and implicit characteristics

Attitudes	Behaviors	Symbols	Explicit Characteristics	Implicit Characteristics
include beliefs (political, ideological, religious, moral), values, general knowledge (empirical and theoretical), opinions, superstitions, and stereotypes	include a wide variety of norms, roles, customs, traditions, habits, practices, and fashions	represent things or ideas; people give them their meaning	• the set of observable acts regularly found in a specific culture • overt customs, observable practices, and typical behavioral responses example: saying "hello" to a stranger	the organizing principles that are inferred to lie behind these regularities on the basis of consistent patterns of explicit behaviors examples: grammar that controls speech, rules of address, hidden norms of bargaining, particular behavioral expectations in a standard situation

Facts to Keep in Mind
- no two cultures are entirely similar or entirely different
- the same cultural cluster can have significant variations and dissimilarities

example: any capitalist society is diverse and stratified, but some Western countries are more stratified than others, whereas others achieve relative equality among their citizens

B. 1. The main concepts in cross-cultural psychology are: (1) it involves the comparative study of at least two cultural groups; (2) it establishes psychological universals which may be common for people in several, or even all, cultures; (3) it defines culture as a set of attitudes, behaviors, and symbols that a particular cultural group shares; (4) it examines the implicit as well as explicit characteristics of cultures.

2. Cross-cultural psychologists have identified human personality traits as a psychological universal. Some of the universal traits include neuroticism, extroversion, openness to experience, agreeableness, and conscientiousness.

3. Students' answers and examples will vary. Any reasonable answer which also demonstrates understanding of the information in the reading is acceptable.

Sentence Focus, p. 236

Paragraph 1: c

Paragraph 2: a, b, d

Paragraph 3: c

Paragraph 4: b

Vocabulary in Context, p. 238

Paragraph 1: b

Paragraph 2: vary

Paragraph 3: c

Paragraph 8: observable

Using the Dictionary, p. 239

Excerpt 1: 1. 3a   2. a

Excerpt 2: clear and easy to see / plain to see / obvious

Write a Summary, p. 240

Students' summaries will vary somewhat but should include the main ideas. A sample summary is as follows:

> Cross-cultural psychologists compare and study how culture affects human psychology, and try to discover the similarities and differences among different cultures. There may be human traits such as personality characteristics that are the same across all cultures. Cross-cultural psychologists define culture as a set of explicit and implicit attitudes, behaviors, and symbols shared by a large group of people and transmitted from one generation to the next. Cross-cultural psychologists keep in mind that cultures are never entirely similar or entirely different, and that there is variation even within a single culture.

Activate Your Knowledge, p. 240

A. Students' work may vary. Any reasonable answer is acceptable but should reflect an understanding of what students have learned so far.

Scanning and Skimming, p. 241

A. Headings:
   Sociobiological Approach
   Sociological Approach
   Ecocultural Approach
   The Integrative Approach

B. sociobiology: a theoretical model that explores the ways in which biological factors affect human behavior and thus lay a natural foundation for human culture

   sociological approach: a general view of human behavior that focuses on broad social structures that influence society as a whole, and subsequently its individuals

   ecocultural approach: a cross-disciplinary approach to studying human behavior which views the individual as inseparable from his or her environmental context

   integrative approach: an approach to studying human behavior which combines the sociobiological, sociological, and ecocultural approaches in studying human behavior

C. 1 and 2. Students' predictions and questions may vary. Anything reasonable is acceptable.

MAIN READING, p. 242

Before You Continue Reading

1. The topic of paragraphs 2 and 3 is the sociobiological approach to studying human behavior, and the main idea is that biological laws of behavior such as natural selection can adequately explain human behavior.

2. The topic of paragraphs 4–6 is the sociological approach to studying human behavior, and the main idea is that there are broad social structures such as tradition or rationality that influence societies and therefore the individuals within the society.

3. The topic of paragraphs 7 and 8 is the ecocultural approach to studying human behavior, and the main idea is that an individual cannot be separated from his or her environmental context, which is part of a larger cultural system that consists of a variety of interdependent settings.

Text Analysis, p. 246

A. Sociobiological Approach

   Key Concepts: The prime goal of human beings is survival; humans of all cultures try to avoid unnecessary pain and eliminate anything that threatens their well-being; Social Darwinism—some organisms are more likely to survive than others; competition steadily develops society by favoring its best-fit members, and over generations, genetic patterns that promote survival become dominant and then form foundations for a culture.

Proponents of This Approach: probably Charles Darwin

Sociological Approach: focuses on social elements such as traditions, which influence society as a whole, and subsequently its individuals

Key Concepts: Society exists objectively, apart from our individual experience; there are particular social forces that shape the behavior of large social groups, and human beings develop and adjust their individual responses in accordance to the demands and pressures of larger social groups and institutions; in societies with simple technologies, strong tradition becomes a powerful moral regulator demanding conformity from the society's members; in modern, wealthy societies, discarded traditions break psychological ties among the individuals, but a huge variety of specializations in the society should make people bond back together.

Proponents of This Approach: Max Weber

Ecocultural Approach: maintains that the individual cannot be separated from his or her environmental context.

Key Concepts: People constantly exchange messages with the environment, thus transforming it and themselves through reciprocal interactions; the individual is seen as a dynamic human being who interacts with and changes the environment; each individual's development takes place within a particular "developmental niche" that can be viewed as a combination of various settings.

Proponents of This Approach: Urie Bronfenbrenner

Integrative Approach: combines the sociobiological, sociological, and ecocultural approaches in studying human behavior

Key Concepts: People are free, active, and rational individuals who are capable of exercising their own will; human motivation, emotion, thought, and reactions cannot be separated from human activity; the presence of and access to resources essential for the individual's well-being largely determine type, scope, and direction of human activities; quality of environment and access to resources may become crucial factors determining many cultural characteristics; people's access to resources affects many aspects of culture and individual behavior; ideas and practices that implement these ideas are inseparable from individual psychology.

Proponents of This Approach: not mentioned

B. Students' work will vary. A diagram might show the four systems as four concentric circles, with the Microsystem as the center circle enclosing the individual, immediate family members, schoolteachers, friends; the next larger circle is the Mesosystem, and should show connections among family, school, and a religious institution such as a church, mosque, or synagogue; the next larger cicle is the Exosystem, and should show the media (e.g., newspapers, TV, radio), extended family members, legal and social organizations (e.g., clubs); the largest circle is the Macrosystem, and should show examples of the customs and beliefs of a particular culture. All the circles should show arrows in two directions, demonstrating interdependence.

D. 1. Proponents of the sociobiological approach explain human behavior as a response to fundamental biological needs such as safety and hunger, which enable the individual to survive.

Answer Key to the Student Book Exercises *103*

2. According to the sociological approach, in some societies such as those with simple technologies, traditions regulate the moral behavior of the society's members, and may force them to think and act in the same ways.

3. According to the ecocultural approach, settings such as the immediate and extended family, school, religious, legal, and social organizations, the media, and the society's customs and beliefs may all mediate the development of the individuals within a culture.

4. A theoretical model helps people study a particular subject by providing a focused and structured way of examining that subject. (Students' examples may vary.) One example is the sociobiological approach, which enables cross-cultural psychologists to examine cultures with regard to the way the individuals within that culture fulfill their biological needs for food, safety, mates, and ways to protect their offspring.

Sentence Focus, p. 248

1. f   2. d   3. b   4. e   5. c   6. a

Vocabulary in Context, p. 249

Paragraph 2: 1. b   2. survive

Paragraph 3: a

Paragraph 6: reason

Paragraph 7: b

Using the Dictionary, p. 250

Excerpt 1: 1. 3   2. a

Excerpt 2: Students' work will vary but should demonstrate an understanding that when people are coerced, they act unwillingly because they act under pressure of force or threats. Students should also demonstrate an understanding that people do experience advantages by thinking and acting in ways their society expects of them, even if they feel coerced. For example, people will be accepted by other members of their society, and they may also be rewarded by other members of their society.

Write a Summary, p. 251

Students' summaries will vary somewhat but should include the main ideas. A sample summary is as follows:

In studying human behavior, cross-cultural psychologists use a variety of models such as the sociobiological approach, the sociological approach, the ecocultural approach, and the integrative approach. Each of these approaches provides a theoretical framework for exploring the factors that influence human behavior, and the ways in which societies and the individuals within societies interact among themselves and with their environment.

Learn and Use Word Forms, p. 252

B. 1. varied
    2. do not rationalize
    3. comparisons
    4. representation
    5. adapt (OR can adapt)
    6. observable
    7. theoretical
    8. interact
    9. symbolic
    10. fluctuate
    11. diverse

Writing Activities, p. 254

1–3. Students' answers may vary but must be accurate and must incorporate vocabulary from the chapter.

Extension Activities, p. 254

1–4. Students' work will vary but must be accurate and must incorporate vocabulary from the chapter and from their research.

Chapter 10

Activate Your Knowledge, p. 257

B. Students' responses will vary. Any reasonable answers are acceptable but should reflect some understanding of the information presented in Chapter 9.

Scanning and Skimming, p. 258

A. Headings:

Sociobiology: A Glance into Evolution

Theories of Social Instincts

Social Science: See the Society First

B. 1. Motivation is a condition (usually internal) that initiates, activates, or maintains an individual's goal-directed behavior.

2. Sociobiologists address the aspect of evolution that concerns natural selection.

3. Social scientists describe preindustrial societies and industrial societies.

C. 1 and 2. Students' predictions and questions may vary. Anything reasonable is acceptable.

INTRODUCTORY READING, p. 259

Before You Continue Reading

1. The topic of paragraph 1 is motivation, and the main idea is that motivation is studied on the basis of a variety of factors including biological, social, economic, and psychological factors.

2. The topic of paragraph 2 is sociobiology, and the main idea is that people are motivated by the biological need to survive, which can be an individual or a collective need.

3. The topic of paragraph 3 is the drawbacks to the sociobiological approach, and the main idea is that the sociobiological approach does not take into account the influence of social, cultural, and religious factors.

4. The topic of paragraph 4 is theories of social instincts, and the main idea is that basic instincts play a universal role in determining human actions, although there is little empirical evidence to support these theories.

Text Analysis, p. 262

(See diagram on next page.)

Text Analysis, p. 262

Motivation
a condition that initiates, activates, or maintains an individual's goal-directed behavior

Theories of Motivation

Sociobiology

- *the origin of human motivation is biological
- people are part of the biological universe
- people need to survive
- *natural selection* is a key interpreter of human behavior
- people who survive pass on their "advantageous" genes to their offspring
- survival can be individual and collective
- people who are unfit or who lack motivation will fail

Social Instincts

- *basic instincts have a universal role in human motivation
- social reflexes are universal and cause humans to act purposefully, overthrow governments, write music, and commit crimes
- Tarde—all human behavior is imitative—envy, vanity, friendship, hatred, love
- Tarde—different social conditions are maintained because of people's natural instict of imitation

Social Science

- Weber—people live in two types of societies: preindustrial (traditional) and industrial (nontraditional)
- in traditional societies, people's desires and actions are viewed as appropriate or not based on customs and rules
- in capitalist societies, people's actions are based on rationality
- Marx—an economic condition of inequality activates human needs
- societies are divided into two large and antagonistic social classes
- the oppressed want their share of resources
- *the oppressors want to keep the status quo

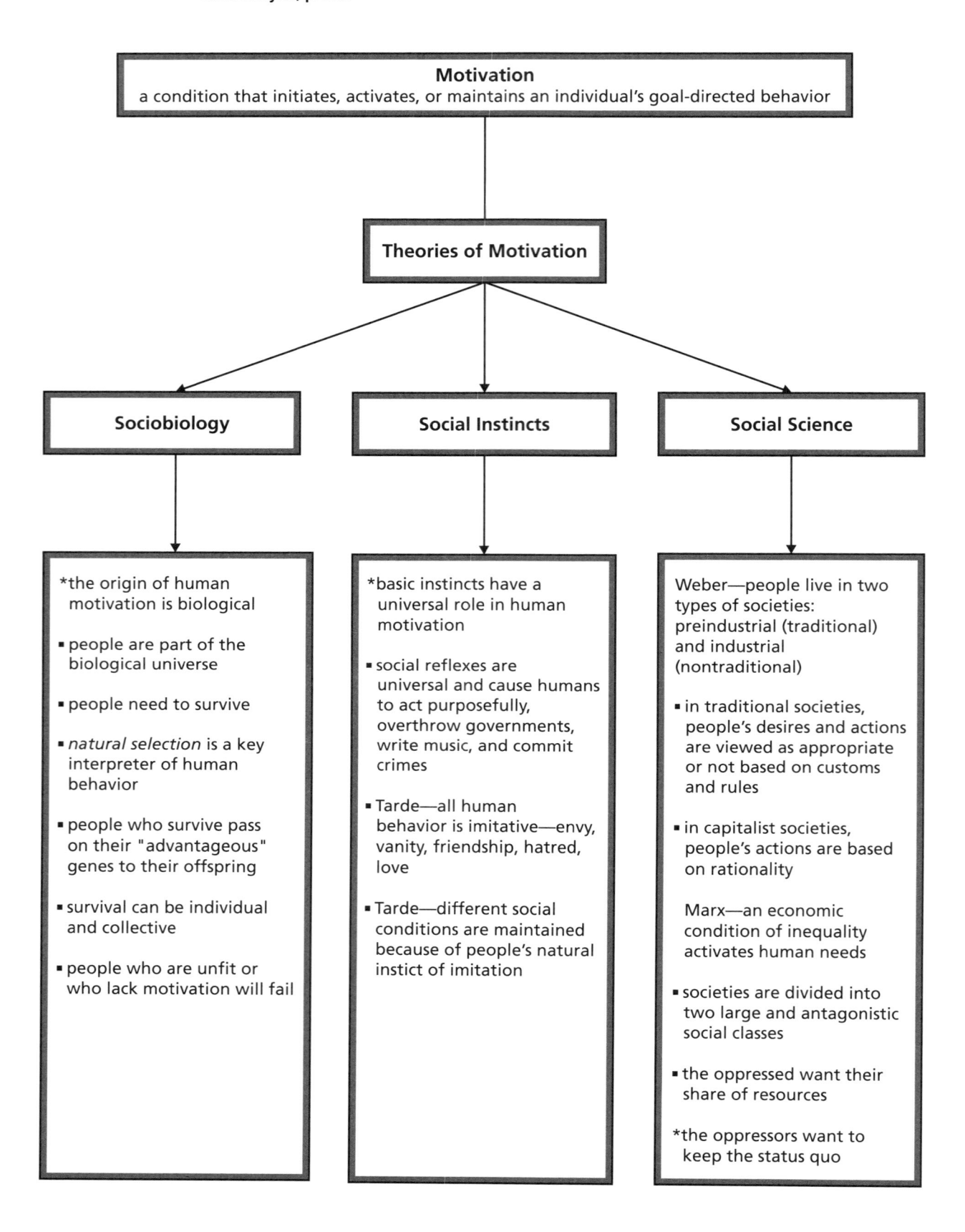

Sentence Focus, p. 264

A. and **B.** Paragraph 3: The sociobiological approach to human motivation <u>generally fails to explain</u> the diversity of human needs and <u>overlooks</u> the influence of social, cultural, and religious factors. However, the "wealth/birth rate" correlation <u>is not proven</u> in rich Arab nations of the Persian basin that continue to have high birth rates.

Paragraph 4: <u>Yet</u> psychological research <u>yields little empirical evidence</u> of the existence of human instincts as "preinstalled" software that causes human action.

Paragraph 7: <u>Despite its attractiveness,</u> Marxism <u>failed to explain</u> many other noneconomic aspects of human motivation. For example, it is easy to show that social equality, unfortunately, does not stop aggression and violence. Similarly, economic inequality does not necessarily cause hostility among people.

C. Students' work will vary but must be reasonable and demonstrate an understanding of the information they have read so far.

Vocabulary in Context, p. 266
Paragraph 1: 1. c 2. a
Paragraph 2: 1. c 2. b 3. a

Using the Dictionary, p. 266
Excerpt 1: 1. 3 2. a
Excerpt 2: b

Write a Summary, p. 268
Students' summaries will vary somewhat but should include the main ideas. A sample summary is as follows:

> Human motivation is studied on the basis of a variety of factors. According to the sociobiological approach, people are motivated by the biological need to survive, and the principle of natural selection plays an important role in human survival. Survival can be an individual or a collective need. This approach, however, does not take into account the diversity of human needs or the influence of social, cultural, and religious factors.

> Human motivation is also explained through other theories which hold that basic instincts play a universal role in determining human actions, although there is little empirical evidence to support these theories. Social scientists view human motivation through the context of preindustrial societies, in which people are motivated by tradition or customs, and industrial societies in which people are motivated by reason.

Activate Your Knowledge, p. 268
A. Students' ordered lists may vary.

Scanning and Skimming, p. 269
A. Headings:

Humanist Theories: Abraham Maslow

Intrinsic and Extrinsic Motivation

Achievement Motivation

Success Motivation

B. 1. Humanist theories focus on human dignity, individual choice, and self-worth.

2. A self-actualizing person needs to satisfy physiological, safety, belonging, love, and esteem needs, and then to fulfill his or her unique potential.

3. These are two types of motivation. Intrinsic motivation engages people in various activities for no apparent reward except the pleasure and satisfaction of the activity itself, whereas extrinsic motivation comes from the external environment, for example praise from others.

C. 1 and 2. Students' predictions and questions may vary. Anything reasonable is acceptable.

MAIN READING, p. 270

Before You Continue Reading

1. The topic of paragraph 1 is need, and the main idea is that human behavior is motivated by both biological and social needs.

2. The topic of paragraphs 2–4 is Maslows's hierarchy of needs, and

the main idea is that people have five levels of needs, which must be satisfied before a person can achieve fulfillment, although the relative strengths of the needs may be culture specific.

3. The topic of paragraph 5 is types of motivation, and the main idea is that people may be motivated by personal pleasure and satisfaction or by external reward.

4. The topic of paragraph 6 is achievement motivation, and the main idea is that achievement is a basic human need.

5. The topic of paragraphs 7–9 is research on achievement motivation, and the main idea is that achievement motivation is learned during childhood and is culture specific.

Text Analysis, p. 274

A. Students' work will vary depending on the formats they chose to use in organizing paragraph 1. A sample is as follows:

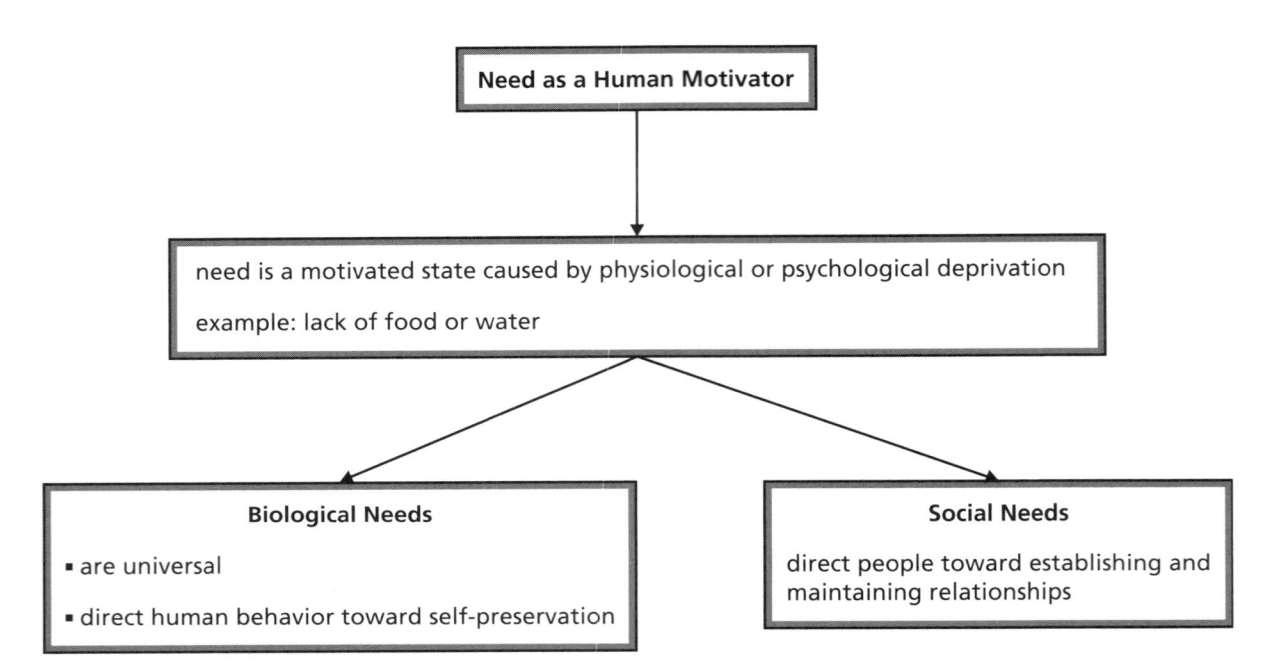

```
┌─────────────────────────────┐
│  Need as a Human Motivator  │
└─────────────────────────────┘
              │
              ▼
┌───────────────────────────────────────────────────────────────────────┐
│ need is a motivated state caused by physiological or psychological    │
│ deprivation                                                           │
│ example: lack of food or water                                        │
└───────────────────────────────────────────────────────────────────────┘
            ↙                                    ↘
┌──────────────────────────────────┐   ┌──────────────────────────────────┐
│      Biological Needs            │   │         Social Needs             │
│ • are universal                  │   │ direct people toward establishing│
│ • direct human behavior toward   │   │ and maintaining relationships    │
│   self-preservation              │   │                                  │
└──────────────────────────────────┘   └──────────────────────────────────┘
```

B. 1. Biological needs are universal, but social needs may not be universal. Biological needs involve survival, but social needs involve relationships with others.

2. As people progress through Maslow's hierarchy of needs, they become less like animals and more humanistic.

3. Humans learn achievement motivation. Two studies, one by McClelland and one by Furnham, demonstrated that levels of achievement motivation are culture specific, and are learned by children.

4. The basic difference between individualist-success motivation and collectivist-success motivation is whether goals are directed to gaining personal goals or goals that benefit members of a group.

C. 1. EM 2. EM 3. EM 4. IM 5. IM 6. IM

Sentence Focus, p. 275

A. Words/Phrases That Indicate a Theory: propose, according to, argue that, could + *verb*, may + *verb*, maintain, suggest, perhaps

Words/Phrases That Indicate Supporting Research: find, show, demonstrate, correlate

B. 2. **SR** David McClelland (1958) demonstrated that achievement motivation is learned during childhood.

108   Answer Key to the Student Book Exercises

3. **T** In one study, Nevis (1983) revised Maslow's hierarchy of needs, and <u>argued</u> that one of the most basic needs of people in communist China is the need to belong, rather than physiological needs.

4. **SR** In a cross-national project that involved more than 12,000 participants, Furnham et al. (1994) also <u>showed a strong relationship</u> between individual achievement motivation and economic growth.

5. **T** Edward Deci (1972) <u>suggested</u> that people engage in such behaviors for two reasons: to obtain cognitive stimulation and to gain a sense of accomplishment, competency, and mastery over the environment.

6. **SR** In Furnham et al.'s <u>study</u> (1994), economic growth <u>correlated with</u> attitudes toward competitiveness.

7. **SR** In one study, <u>it was found</u> that educated American children displayed a stronger capacity for delaying their expectations for an immediate reward than less educated children, who showed the opposite trend (Doob, 1971).

8. **T** Particular social norms <u>may be linked</u> to achievement motivation.

9. **SR** A study of American, Polish, and German children (Boehnke et al., 1989) <u>showed</u> that in all three samples girls preferred intrinsic motives more frequently than boys.

10. **T** <u>Perhaps</u> achievement-oriented motivation was part of the socialization of the boys in the studied nations (Boehnke et al., 1989).

Vocabulary in Context, p. 277

Paragraph 1: b

Paragraph 3 1. a   2. fulfill

Paragraph 5: c

Using the Dictionary, p. 277

Excerpt 1: 1. 1   2. c

Excerpt 2: a

Write a Summary, p. 279

Students' summaries will vary somewhat but should include the main ideas. A sample summary is as follows:

Human behavior is motivated by biological and social needs. Abraham Maslow proposed a five-level hierarchy of needs that begins with biological needs and rises to sociological needs. People must satisfy these needs in ascending order to achieve personal fulfillment. People may be motivated by intrinsic factors such as personal pleasure and satisfaction, or by external factors such as praise or other rewards. Still another factor is achievement motivation, which is another basic human need, although this, too, is culture specific. In fact, success motivation is also culture specific. Each society values individualist-success motivation, which leads to the attainment of personal goals, or to collectivist-success motivation. In this way, the individual contributes to the goals of the group.

Learn and Use Word Forms, p. 279

B. 1. diversity
   2. survival
   3. achievement
   4. do not imitate
   5. self-actualization
   6. stimuli (OR stimulus)
   7. motivate
   8. initiate
   9. socialized
   10. fulfilling

Writing Activities, p. 281

1–3. Students' answers may vary but must be accurate and must incorporate vocabulary from the chapter.

Extension Activities, p. 282

1–4. Students' work will vary but must be accurate and must incorporate vocabulary from the chapter and from their research.

Websites

The last Extension Activity in the Student Book gives students key words to use in an Internet search. Websites are given here for further research. Since websites frequently change, become obsolete, or expire, be sure to check each one before recommending it to your students.

Unit 1

Public Broadcasting System:
http://www.pbs.org/wgbh/aso/databank/entries/bhskin.html

Valdosta State University, Valdosta, Georgia:
http://chiron.valdosta.edu/whuitt/col/behsys/operant.html

B. F. Skinner Foundation: http://www.bfskinner.org

Theory into Practice Database: http://tip.psychology.org/skinner.html

Ohio Wesleyan University Online, Delaware, Ohio:
http://go.owu.edu/~deswartz/procedures/habituation.html

Brainviews, Ltd.: http://www.brainviews.com/abFiles/AniLearn.htm
(Visit the home page and choose from the menu.)

Konrad Lorenz Institute: http://www.kli.ac.at
(Visit the home page and choose from the menu.)

Nature Publishing Group: http://www.nature.com
(Type a key word or phrase in the Search box, or select from the menu.)

United States Environmental Protection Agency: http://www.epa.gov
(Type a key word or phrase in the Search box, or select from the menu.)

Unit 2

Indiana University, Bloomington, Indiana:
http://www.indiana.edu/~workshop/wsl/org.html

UNESCO (United Nations Educational, Scientific and Cultural Organization):
http://www.unesco.org
(Select a theme from the menu, especially *Social Sciences* and *Culture*).

University of Manitoba, Canada's Department of Anthropology, Winnipeg:
http://www.umanitoba.ca/anthropology/kintitle.html

Power Source, Sugarland, Texas:
http://www.powersource.com/gallery/people/sequoyah.html

Sequoyah Museum, Vonore, Tennessee: http://www.sequoyahmuseum.org

Cherokee Nation: http://www.cherokee.org

Unit 3

School of Mathematics and Statistics, University of St Andrews, Scotland:
http://www-history.mcs.st-andrews.ac.uk/Mathematicians/Copernicus.html

The University of Tennessee at Martin, The Internet Encyclopedia of Philosophy:
http://www.utm.edu/research/iep/a/aristotl.htm

University of California, Berkeley, Museum of Paleontology:
http://www.ucmp.berkeley.edu/history/aristotle.html

School of Mathematics and Statistics, University of St Andrews, Scotland:
http://www-history.mcs.st-andrews.ac.uk/Mathematicians/Galileo.html

Electronic Studio, Rice University, Houston, Texas:
http://es.rice.edu/ES/humsoc/Galileo/Catalog/Files/galilei_gal.html

The Science Museum, Florence, Italy: http://galileo.imss.firenze.it

Contemporary College Physics Simulation Library:
http://www.walterfendt.de/ph11e/ncradle.htm

School of Law, University of Missouri, Kansas City, Missouri:
http://www.law.umkc.edu/faculty/projects/ftrials/galileo/recantation.html

Unit 4

Uffizi Museum, Florence: www.uffizi.it

Web Gallery of Art: (This website has the works of many artists, listed by name.)
http://www.wga.hu

Christus Rex et Redemptor Mundi: (This website has color illustrations of the *Très Riches Heures du Duc de Berry*.)
http://www.christusrex.org/www2/berry/index.html

InterArt: http://www.inter-art.com/en

Oxford University:
http://www.robots.ox.ac.uk/~vgg/projects/SingleView/examples.html
(This website has an animation of a three-dimensional model of Masaccio"s *The Trinity*. Go to the website. Click on *Some Examples*, then click on *La Trinitá*, and follow the instructions.)

National Palace Museum, Taipei, Taiwan:
http://www.npm.gov.tw/main/fmain_en.htm

Museum of Fine Arts, Boston: http://www.mfa.org
(Click on *Collections*, then click on *Art of Asia, Oceania, and Africa*. Then click on *Chinese Painting*. Use the Search mode to locate paintings of the Southern Song Dynasty, Xia Gui, etc.)

This website lists a number of other websites on Chinese Calligraphy:
http://www.chinapage.com/callig1.html

The Friesian School website: http://www.friesian.com/confuci.htm

Unit 5

Center for Cross-Cultural Research: http://www.ac.wwu.edu/~culture/readings.htm

"Intercultural Relations.com": http://www.interculturalrelations.com

Valdosta State University, Valdosta, Georgia:
http://chiron.valdosta.edu/whuitt/col/regsys/maslow.html
(Maslow's hierarchy clarified)

York University, Canada: http://psychclassics.yorku.ca/Maslow/motivation.htm
(original Maslow article)

Wikipedia: http://en.wikipedia.org/wiki/Economic_sociology ("Economic Sociology" with links)

University of Chicago, Chieagon, Illinois:
http://ssr1.uchicago.edu/PRELIMS/Theory/weber.html (Society for Social Research)

Australian National University, Canberra:
http://www.anu.edu.au/polsci/marx/classics/manifesto.html (Full copy of Karl Marx/Friedrich Engle's "Communist Manifesto".)

Washington State University, Pullman:
http://www.wsu.edu:8080/~wldciv/world_civ_reader/world_civ_reader_2/marx.html ("Communist Manifesto" with notes, explanations and linked definitions)

Shippensburg University, Shippensberg, Pennsylvania:
http://www.ship.edu/~cgboeree/sociobiology.html (treatise on Sociobiology)

Wikipedia: http://en.wikipedia.org/wiki/Sociobiology ("Sociobiology" with links)

University of California, Chico:
http://www.ecst.csuchico.edu/~jorgense/handbook.htm (Intrinsic motivation explained vis-a-vis business organization, etc.)

University of Rhode Island, Kingston:
http://www.cba.uri.edu/scholl/Notes/Sources_Motivation.htm

PEARSON
Longman

ISBN 0-13-140201-3